Step by step,
the longest march can be won,
can be won.
Many stones can form an arch;
singly none;
singly none.
And by union, what we will
Can be accomplished still.
Drops of water turn a mill;
Singly none;
Singly none.

Words from the Preamble to the
Constitution of the United Mine
Workers, adapted for a freedom song.

Published for the Fayette County Fund

STEP BY STEP

EVOLUTION AND OPERATION OF THE CORNELL STUDENTS'
CIVIL-RIGHTS PROJECT IN TENNESSEE, SUMMER, 1964

by Fayette County Project Volunteers

W · W · NORTON & COMPANY · INC · NEW YORK

ISBN 978-0-393-00317-8

Printed in the United States of America

1 2 3 4 5 6 7 8 9 0

*Dedicated to our friends in Fayette County, Tennessee,
and to all others who fight for freedom, now.*

The summer volunteers

Daniel Beagle
David Boesel
Helen Brosius
Douglas and
  Lorna Caulkins
Richard V. Denenberg
Douglas F. Dowd
Nadine Felton
Mary Ella Fisher
Robert and Vicki Gabriner
George Gibian
William Griffen
Joe and Patricia Griffith
Douglas Hainline
Timothy Hall
Charles and Rowena Haynie
John Heawood
Marcia Heinemann
Gregory Herzog
Richard Hughes
David Jette
Thomas Kapnar
Herbert Kelsey

David Kotelchuck
David Kubrin
Elizabeth and
  Nicholas Lawrence
Neil Lowry
Judith Miller
William Murrell
Ralph Naden
Mary D. Nichols
Daniel Packtor
Ronald Schneider
Paul Seidel
Richard Shaper
Alice and Daniel Snowman
James Snyder
Augusta Sousa
Gerald Surette
Richard Valenstein
Neil Varian
Daniel Watt
Fred Weaver
Burton Weiss
Charles Woll

Contents

Photographs by Nick Lawrence

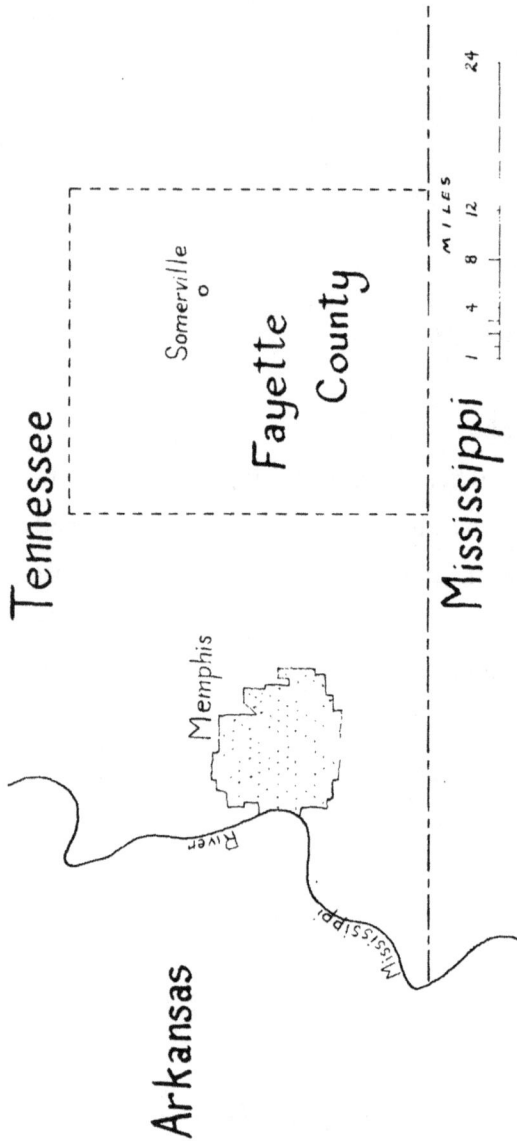

Preface

This is the story of the Cornell-Tompkins County Committee for Free and Fair Elections in Fayette County, Tennessee. The Committee, which developed and carried out the Fayette County Project, was formed at Cornell University in the winter of 1964. It raised money and volunteers to spend the summer of 1964 in Fayette County in civil-rights work. About fifty volunteers spent their summers in this way, most of them staying in the county six to eight weeks. The interest of the project lies not so much in what it did, as in who did it, and how the project was developed. It was developed and financed by the Cornell community, including the townspeople of the area. It is the belief of the Fayette County Project members that their experience both can and should be repeated at other college campuses. This book is in part a handbook on how to go about doing just that.

Chapter 1

And if not now . . . ?

Justice is a power; and if it cannot create, it will destroy." Written long ago, and in another land, this admonition might have been coined yesterday, by Martin Luther King, Aaron Henry, a mother in Harlem, a sharecropper in Alabama—or by Malcolm X. The fight for civil rights, for human decency, must soon register decisive victories, or all will suffer. The fight will see no armistice —only triumph, or disaster. The forces pressing for and against civil rights accelerate, and all Americans, like it or not, are caught up in the swift currents of the struggle. In a handful of years, the creative or the destructive outcome of that struggle will have been determined.

Whatever else it may have produced, the civil-rights movement has yielded tension, confusion, and agonizing paradoxes. Conscience finds consciousness to move against injustice, *and* latent Northern racism combines with Southern tradition to shore up the walls of fear. Negroes, North and South, win improvements in their lives, *and* frustration, desperation, and anger mount in the Negro community. The fight for civil rights has bogged down, say some; *and,* say others, it moves too fast. Money and workers to aid the movement multiply, *and* there is a desperate shortage of money and people in the movement.

Faced with these and other dualities, those who identify with the movement—those to whom this book is ad-

11

dressed—too often find themselves mesmerized, their hopes pinned on the merely hoped-for actions of others, somewhere, their fears nameless and looming. What can *I* do? becomes not so much a query as a sigh of despair. Is it that there are too few Americans concerned with civil rights, too few who see the Negro's battle as their own? Perhaps. Probably. But more to the point is the fact that so many hundreds of thousands, even so many millions of Americans possess, after all, the requisites of decency, courage, and will, to work actively for civil rights, but can find no answers to the problems of how? where? when? with whom? We face a tragedy not so much of evil, although there is evil enough, but of paralysis. It is all the more tragic for being so; all the more tragic because it need not be so.

Students, faculty, and townspeople at Cornell University and in and around Ithaca, New York, found answers to the questions just posed. They did so in the "good old American tradition" of making up their own answers, by developing a civil-rights project of their own. The name of the project, which continues, is as awkward as it is descriptive: the Cornell-Tompkins County Committee for Free and Fair Elections in Fayette County, Tennessee. The project had at least two critical aspects to it. First, the "county-to-county" dimensions of its aims reduced what had been enormous and diffuse—the civil-rights movement—to a matter small enough to be easily intelligible and feasible, while retaining its importance. All that was needed was the will, and some money. Second, Fayette County was no stranger to civil-rights work by the time it attracted our attention; that was why our attention was drawn to it.

For several years, the Negroes of the county had doggedly and bravely carried on the difficult and dangerous work of voter registration. Alone, it had become clear in

1963, they could not go much further. It is not too much to say that the tensions and the possibilities of Fayette County in 1963 were much like those more generally of the civil-rights struggle in the nation as a whole: too much had been done to turn back, or even to stop; nor was there any intention of doing so. However, without help from "outsiders," frustrations would mount and failures lead to internal rifts. The future would become one of despair, if not of retrogression.

As for the nation, so for Fayette County: on-the-spot human and financial resources for continued progress have been and remain inadequate. This is so for the reason that much is being done already; and, as each new step toward change is taken, horizons both broaden and rise—*more* must be done, and that which must be done becomes more complex. Consequently, between the needs of those who fight and the resources of those who would help, the gap widens; it could become an abyss swallowing the hopes of both.

The Fayette County project required six to eight weeks of living in the county by the volunteers, mostly students from Cornell University. The project was their "how." The summer in the county was their "when" and "where." A relatively small number of Negro leaders in Fayette County constituted their "with whom." By the end of the summer, the "with whom" had mounted to thousands, and the Negroes had their own political organization. Their need for outside help continues, but now they and we can accomplish more substantial ends, with fewer people from outside.

Not everyone can devote a summer to civil-rights work, nor were the summer workers the only ones to find answers to questions of how to become involved. Initially, it was estimated that the project would need about five thousand dollars to support the summer volunteers in the county, and to get them down and back. Over fifteen thousand dollars was collected, and ultimately all of it was needed. The money came from contributions, ranging from the nickels and dimes of school children to large checks from their parents. Most of the money was collected in the vicinity of Ithaca, but several thousand dollars were raised by meetings initiated by Cornell people in other areas (New York City, Lancaster, Pa., Cambridge, Buffalo, for instance). The techniques of collection included the making and sale of a record, fund-raising meetings, personal letters, articles in newspapers and magazines, and concerts.

What was surprising, to recipients and contributors alike, was not that money was given by all these people, for some had of course given before. It was that so much came forth, from so many, and so easily—with so little urging. What was the secret of this generous response? The answer to that question will unfold in detail in Chapter III. The answer is simple, rather than profound. It is that the nature of the project allowed those to whom we appealed to identify with it. Our financial supporters, no less than the volunteers, were able to see the project as "their" project. The Fayette County Project was one that could be watched as it grew; its purposes were limited and plain, but no less urgent for that; it was a project whose members were, so to speak, visible. It was a project, put differently, whose success or failure, whose dangers and challenges, involved people from the community whose support was sought, as well as those in the community receiving help. Why the response to this kind of immediacy should differ so in magnitude from, say, an appeal for funds for CORE, or financial support for the Mississippi project* is not a matter which we feel either

* And we need not speculate on the difference, for appeals were made both before and after the Fayette Project at Cornell, to the

14

can or need be dealt with fully here. What seems relevant, however, is some combination of feelings deriving from a sense of community, of pride and responsibility; of personal attachment to the volunteers—in short, from a complex of proprietary and "family" feelings. What we learned in this respect was one of the most important of the many lessons of the Fayette County Project. We are confident that a similar approach in other communities would be equally rewarding.

The intent of the chapters to follow is to pass on *all* that we learned, to detail the step-by-step development and operations of the Fayette County Project, in the hope that others who possess the will may find here a key to unlock the door that separates ends from means. There is no lack of areas, South or North, where individual and organized volunteers are badly needed, or where funds are badly needed. What is missing is a way of bringing together those who need help and those who would provide it, if only they knew how.* Ours was one way; it can be used as a model, with appropriate variations, for many others.

The Fayette County Project had many steps to it, each requiring the others. Each of these steps will be examined in detail in ensuing chapters, but here a quick look may be useful. There was first the recognition that help from our area was badly needed in another. We gained that understanding from three Cornell students who participated in voter-registration work in the county in the summer of 1963. Second, a feasible plan was needed. That was worked out in the fall of 1963, and it required meetings of people from Ithaca with people

---

same people, even by the same people, with slighter results.

  * The several civil-rights organizations have provided a list of areas and projects requiring assistance, and that list makes up the Appendix.

from the county and from experienced civil-rights organizations. Third, the project had to be publicized and developed in Ithaca; money had to be raised, and personnel had to be found and trained. Fourth, hopes, plans, and work had to come together in Fayette County in what proved to be a complicated and occasionally dangerous summer. Fifth, the work of the summer had to become a new first step, in a process of change that goes on still, and whose end is unpredictable—either in nature or in time.

"The work of the summer . . . " The work of the summer was an achievement, and a great one, as is most likely to be true for other groups in other places and other summers. But it is vital to make a proper distinction, in such work, between achievement and failure, lest the one be mistaken for the other. In the area of civil rights, more than elsewhere, it is to easy to mistake substantial achievement for failure, too easy for the illusion of success to be taken as genuine achievement. The problems and the possibilities are very different, and the measuring rods must be different.

Did the Fayette County Project "succeed"? The election of the summer was lost, and badly. The schools of the county were, and they remain, totally segregated, and the condition of those for Negroes is scandalous. Unemployment, real and disguised, is rife. For Negroes who can find work, wages and hours are worse than those fought for in the 1930's—wages average below forty cents an hour, and the working day often lasts fourteen hours. All public and private facilities are separate, and unequal, and there are few community facilities of any sort for Negroes, except churches. There is no public transportation, except school buses. And in this latter respect the conditions of the county are symbolized; the school buses are separate and dangerously unequal, in a horrifying way—white drivers do not stop for halted Negro school buses, despite the law. And the Negro school children are packed into the buses like sardines, with sometimes ninety children (by actual count) in a bus designed for thirty.

Those were the conditions in Fayette County when our project began, and those conditions persist to this day. Yet, we and the Negroes of Fayette County won a victory in the summer of 1964. It was a victory measurable in terms of an erupting sense of injustice, an exploding sense of possibilities. It was a victory resting in the new solidarity and mutual respect of black and white, new for both black and white, wondrous for both black and white.

The Negroes of the county knew, of course, that they lived under a system of repression, of injustice. But the repression had been successful enough to keep from them the details. Only dimly did the Negroes of the county perceive their rights; their knowledge of law approached zero; they knew little about how to move from wrong to right. Most had the dignity, some had the will, but none had the power. We extended our strength, and now the Negroes know, and what they know they hold in their feelings, in their spirit, in their daily activities, in their now substantial political organization, in their new libraries and literary schools—in their plans.

The life of the county is now changing rapidly, and everyone in it, whether black or white, knows it. Not for long will schools remain segregated, not for long will traditional ills be tolerated. One saw that on August 6, 1964, on election day, the day the election was lost so badly. An hour before the polls opened, about three thousand legally registered Negroes stood in line, where fewer than sixty had stood in 1959. They stood there without our help, that day. We could have left the county the day before the election, and their own organization would have done the work of the day, as indeed it did. The victory of the summer was in the exultant faces of the Negroes of the county.

It was a victory wrought not by unusually gifted people, but by common people who took thought, and acted. The achievements of the Fayette County Project can be repeated and extended by others, and elsewhere. It is the context, not the uncommon characteristics of those who work within it, that makes for the achievement. Not that we made no mistakes. Project plans sometimes went awry, and individuals on the project made errors of omission and commission. These mistakes, which will be discussed later, need not be repeated by others, nor are they likely to be when their nature is known. The worst mistake of all is not to try, to find no good answer to the ancient question, "And if not now, when?"

Because the intent of this book is the stimulation and instruction of others who would take a more active part in civil-rights work, one further point should be made, before pushing into details. The point is not without irony. It would appear that those who volunteer for such work must have a commitment strong enough to undergo sacrifices, at least in prospect—sacrifices of time, income, comfort, well-being, even of safety. In fact, however, those who have done civil-rights work all testify to the enrichment, the enhancement, the greater meaning of their lives. Those who fight in this struggle make no sacrifice, need no sympathy; they are to be envied.

Chapter II

The reason why:
Fayette County, Tennessee

LIKE SO MUCH of the South, Fayette County is lovely
to see. The land is mostly flat, but it is green, with here
and there a gentle hill. There are creeks, rivers, ponds,
and lakes sprinkled over the county. The highways are
bordered by deep ditches profuse with wildly climbing
vines, or they are lined with graceful and diverse trees.
The redness of the soil joins the lush greenery to promise
abundance. One can imagine the pleasure, even the excitement, of the pioneers as they first viewed the landscape
of Fayette County.

But that was long ago. Today, the physical beauty of
the land is all but obscured by the ugliness of the society.
The contrast is aptly suggested by a closer look at the
lovely ponds and lakes; the waters are brackish, and they
abound in poisonous snakes. There are few swimming
holes in Fayette County, and none but mudholes for
Negroes. The rich soil has been worn out by over a cen-
tury of misuse; it now requires heavy doses of fertilizer
to be cultivable. Much of the once-productive land lies
smothered in rank weeds.

The nature of the population—something under thirty
thousand, with two Negroes for every white—suggests
much concerning the county's history, its economics, its
culture. It is old plantation and slave country. It is Faulk-
ner country. The county's history mingles imperceptibly
with that of the delta lands of Mississippi, with which it

shares its southern boundary.

Socially, the county is more a part of Mississippi than of Tennessee. Both the economic and the social life of the county mix the populations of Fayette County and northern Mississippi. Some Fayette County Negroes attend church in Mississippi, and vice versa. Many of the whites who work in the few and tiny factories of the county commute daily from their homes in Mississippi. At night and by cloud, the numerous bootlegging operations of the county—dry by local and profitable option—enjoy the advantages of the nearness and gracious corruptibility of also-dry Mississippi and its petty officialdom.

In their assumptions, outlook, and behavior, the white citizens of Fayette County are more Mississippian than Tennessean. The Supreme Court's "all deliberate speed" may have provoked laughs, or violence, or vacant stares, in Fayette County; it did not move the whites in any other manner.

But Fayette County is *in* Tennessee, whose elections laws and whose government, whatever their defects when placed against the American ideal, are a substantial advance over the ideals as well as the facts of the Mississippi custom. The tension in the county owes much to the fact that although it is a political unit of the Border South, it lives within the realities of the Deep South.

Tension has been heightened in recent years not merely by changes made elsewhere in the South, but also because Fayette County adjoins Shelby County, which means that Memphis is less than an hour away by auto. Negroes in Memphis have voted for many years;* they

* As a result of a pleasing irony. In years past Boss Crump "gave" Memphis Negroes the right to vote, for the reasons and with the techniques of the city political machine. When he was deposed, in large part through the efforts of the late Estes Kefauver, the Negroes retained the vote; it is now used in a different manner.

now hold the balance of power in city and congressional elections. Memphis schools have slowly but steadily begun to desegregate, and peacefully so. When Fayette County Negroes migrate, they move first to Memphis; often, they return on Sundays. Some return from Memphis, or Chicago, or Cincinnati, or Louisville, for good—some because they prefer the openhanded tyranny of the rural South to the hypocrisy of the urban ghetto, some because the warmth of a family existence pulls them back from the chilly impersonality of the city, some few because they know of and are heartened by the political stirrings in the county. Those who return are often "city slickers," and often patronizing. Whatever the reason, whatever the attitude, whatever the length of stay, those who have been away bring back knowledge of a different and a partially, if not always a wholly, better world. Also, Memphis has a "Negro" radio station, that is listened to in the county throughout its broadcast day.

Pushed by harsh circumstance, and pulled by consciousness of a better, if none too good, world of fact and rhetoric, the Negroes of Fayette County fight toward the realization of "the dream."

The economics of Fayette County are much like those in the other 137 counties in the nation where Negroes outnumber whites; they are the economics of cheap agricultural labor. The county is almost fully rural—much more so, for example, than most of Mississippi. Its economic health is determined still by the cotton crop and the cotton market—although soybeans, okra, and purple-hulled peas are also grown and marketed, with less but growing emphasis. Hence, the productive energies of the people, and much of their conversation, center around cotton.

Cotton has been not so much king, as dictator. It remains so, if with an influence that steadily declines. Re-

cently, the county has seen the emergence of a newcomer —a cattle industry. The latter grows in part because it is profitable; but also, and perhaps in greater part, it grows because it virtually eliminates the need for Negro labor. "The landowners are pushing off the black-faced men and putting on the white-faced cattle, who don't give them no trouble," was one Negro's way of putting it. Beef cattle farms, mechanization of planting and harvesting, the use of chemicals to eliminate the need for cotton "chopping," these changes all add up to a simple, if unsettling, fact— the county's whites have belatedly begun to move in promising economic directions, but more because of the political restiveness of the Negroes than because of a sudden conversion to economic rationality. In one way or another, the Negro in Fayette County, as in the entire South, has dominated the economy. In the past this was because of his low price; today it is because of his growing refusal "to be treated that-a-way."

Fayette County is one of the three largest in Tennessee. It is about seven hundred square miles in area. There is a reasonably good network of blacktop roads, which serve the economic needs of the white farmers well. But most of the people in the county, that is, the Negroes, do not live on the sides of those, or even of the gravel-topped roads. The Negroes live on the sides and ends of dirt roads—deeply rutted and impassably muddy after even an hour's rain; narrow, and risky for both car and driver at anything above a snail's pace. As the project was developing, in Ithaca, our field director, who knew the county, told us that one way to get to safety when chased was to get to a dirt road. Then one would know he was in Negro territory, and therefore safe. Although that did not prove to be true in all cases, it served as a useful rule of thumb.

The largest town in Fayette County is Somerville, the

county seat. The town has barely 2,500 souls, spread thinly in the area widening away from the courthouse square. Somerville can be identified from miles away by day or night by its very high water tower. At night the project workers found some rueful humor in the large, bright neon cross atop the water tower, and appreciated the wry observation of local Negroes that "the whites of Fayette County are about as far from real Christian feeling as that cross is from the ground."

The rural quality of life in the county is reflected wherever the eye, the mind, the nose, the ear may turn. The county has a few small factories, which altogether hire under six hundred workers, perhaps five per cent of them Negroes. In one instance, the Negro employees are used part time in the factory owner's cotton fields, which adjoin the factory building.

The county is preindustrial. Time is measured—or left unmeasured—in the old way. The air smells that way; the incessant crowing of roosters, grunts of the hogs, mooing of the cows, sound that way. There may be a handful of buildings more than two stories tall, but one would be hard put to find them. The county is rural, too, in the important social role played by sitting and talking, by gossip, and in its preoccupation with other people's doings. Our kind of project would not have worked so well in an industrial area; we were much helped by the proclivity to sit and talk and listen. We learned that an eight o'clock meeting means that the audience will arrive at nine; but if it was true that meetings always began very late, it was equally true that nobody was ever in a hurry to leave early.

Again, typical of the rural South, Fayette County possesses one further characteristic of vital importance in the movement: the Negroes are much dominated by religion. That means, of course, Christianity of a funda-

mentalist variety, Baptist or Methodist, and totally segra-
gated churches. The religion is one of Christian love, and
is communicated by the word more than the Book, as
would be expected in a region marked by widespread
illiteracy. It is a religion of charismatic preachers, and
hymns, a religion of active involvement of preacher with
his flock. It is the religion suggested by James Baldwin
in *Go Tell It on the Mountain.*

The church, and there seems to be hundreds of tiny
churches in the county, is by custom and by default
the prime meeting place; there are virtually no other us-
able community facilities. Meetings of Negroes for purposes transcending or opposing the interests of the whites
would not be allowed in the schools. The church is the
meeting place for minds, and hearts, and messages. It
was our meeting place, too.

Rural America has no monopoly on poverty, nor is
rural poverty confined to the South. But the poverty of
the rural South is made all the more grinding by its context. That context is one combining a long-run decline in
the incomes to be gained from cash-crop agriculture with
the heavy chains of racism. There are, one need not say,
poor whites. Their plight can be severe, but there are
ways out of it that are inaccessible to their black counterparts. The ·poor white, after all, is white. He can send
his children to a school which, if it falls short of the
ideal, at least reflects the best intentions of those who
hold power in the South. Not so, of course, the Negro.
The poor white can often find a job in the new factories
of the South; or if he leaves the South, he can move up a
notch elsewhere. The Negro's job opportunities in the
South are confined by racial barriers, limited by lack of
training and education; and when he leaves the South,
the Negro is more often than not leaving a rural back-
wash for an urban ghetto.

The young Negroes do leave Fayette County. An extremely high percentage of the Negroes of the county are very old or very young. Whatever their age, those who remain find themselves almost exclusively occupied in agricultural work, work which even without racism would yield terribly low incomes. The average Negro is able to find perhaps four full months of work a year in the county. He puts in a twelve-to-fourteen-hour day in the fields—he, and his wife, and his children. Whether as a sharecropper, a renter, or an owner, the average family's annual dollar income is measured in hundreds—this, for the very large families of the county, families that commonly number from eight to sixteen children.

The education of the young does more to demoralize than to train the children. Unfortunate though the name of the Negro high school may be—it is called the Fayette County Training School, whereas that for the whites has the more usual name of High School—even that is a misnomer. Teachers and students pool their ignorance in a pitiful mockery of a "college preparatory" curriculum. For example, selected seniors might well be taught something called French by a teacher who has never even spoken to a person who could speak French, by a teacher who has not really, if at all, studied French herself. The resulting dialect is completely incomprehensible, as is the purpose of the training.

So, for the young, abundant time is wasted—except when the fields call. School schedules for Negro grade and high-school children are different from those for the whites, so that the Negro children will be available to meet the rhythm of seed and plant. For example, school for Negroes is in session in July, while the red flower of the cotton plant turns to white. In September, while white children attend school, Negro children pick the cotton. The result of all this is predictable; the graduate of the

Fayette County Training School is less well-educated than a grade-school graduate from a representative Northern community. The educational malnutrition of the Negro children would be disgrace enough were it to stop at that. But to malnutrition there must be added the poisoning and crippling of the child, whose understanding of the mind's possibilities is systematically distorted and permanently stunted.

School buildings and houses for Negroes are much alike. They are, mostly, shacks—rickety in structure, badly illuminated, lacking central heating or plumbing, served by wells dangerously close to outhouses. Anticipating these conditions, the project volunteers—all of whom were to live with Negro families—took shots for diseases that one would prefer to think no longer existed in America; and even so, a few fell ill from drinking the water.

A cheerful note—electricity is abundant. In this TVA area, there seem to be no homes without a lightbulb or a radio. Once in a while, there is a television set, frequently an electric fan, sometimes a freezer. Through the ever-present radio and the occasional television set, the Negroes of the county are enabled to escape the purely white southern viewpoint, able to hear national news through network facilities—to hear the magic word "Chet?"—and to gain a glimpse of another facet of the American way of life. In an area where better than half, perhaps three quarters, of the people are illiterate, the banalities of radio and television provide a vital stimulus —perhaps the most damning commentary one could make on the quality of life in Fayette County.

The dreariness and the horror of the picture is unhappily a familiar one; further details are unnecessary. But a question arises. How, from this oppressed and crippled society, did or could a vigorous civil-rights movement emerge? The answer is a compound of time, place, and circumstance, of course; but it must include as well the precious ingredients of courage and will, and the endurance of the Negroes of Fayette County.

The story begins with just that oppression of mind and body described above. Misery, existing in a time when hope and promise were daily announced in the nation, led to a quickening of spirit. Its first obvious manifestation in the county came in 1959, and it came in the form of the first voter-registration drive by and for Negroes in the county's history.

It all started oddly enough. In the spring of 1959, a Negro was tried in the county court for an alleged offense having nothing to do with civil rights. The man was represented by a prominent Negro civil-rights attorney from Memphis, there being no lawyers in the county who would represent a Negro in court. As the all-white jury was in the process of being selected, the Negro attorney, J. F. Estes, questioned the justice of a trial by a jury in an area where the defendant was denied the right to vote, let alone to have one of his color on the jury. "Why, we got nothing against niggers voting," said a white in the court. "All they gotta do is come to the courthouse and register." The tongue-in-cheek remark was made in the presence of a number of young Fayette County Negroes. They began to talk about registering, throughout the county; soon a large number of Negroes was prepared to register. With the help of the attorney, the Negroes formed the Fayette County Civic and Welfare League. The League has served more than one useful purpose since 1959—and it has also split into two factions—but it was formed originally to foster voter registration.

What began with some hesitancy, even uncertainty as to its purpose, was quickly transformed into a militant and determined movement. The transforming agent was the unbending resistance of the white citizens. Each step taken by the Negroes was met by increasingly vigorous reactions from the whites, in turn promoting more awareness and stronger wills in the Negro community.° First, most characteristically, and persisting still, the whites made the registration process as difficult and as frustrating as possible for the hundreds of Negroes who made the attempt.

Voter registration can occur only at one place, the courthouse, on one day a week, Wednesday—for Negroes (we have much evidence to support the belief that whites are less constrained). In a county as large as Fayette, with people as poor as the Negroes there, it is something of an effort even to get to the courthouse; and it is most frustrating for a few hundred people to stand in line a whole day, only to have all but a score prevented from registering by deliberate slowdown tactics. Despite all, the registration went on, week after week, and it was successful enough in numbers to prompt the whites to apply another tactic in the fall of 1959, the "all-white primary."

Tennessee election laws are liberal and explicit. To register and vote, one need only be twenty-one years old and a resident of the state (and of the county in which one votes). There is no literacy test, no poll tax, no mention of color. The all-white primary, and so it was described by the county election officials, was patently illegal. But to have it declared so in this, as in so many

° One attempt of the whites was successful; namely, to split the League. Using their legal and financial coercion, the whites were able to induce one of the early Negro leaders to split off from the League, and to lead him to use his (thereby much dwindled) influence in the Negro community in classic Uncle Tom fashion. The League in its militant wing continues now as the "Original Fayette County Civic and Welfare League," led by John McFerren.

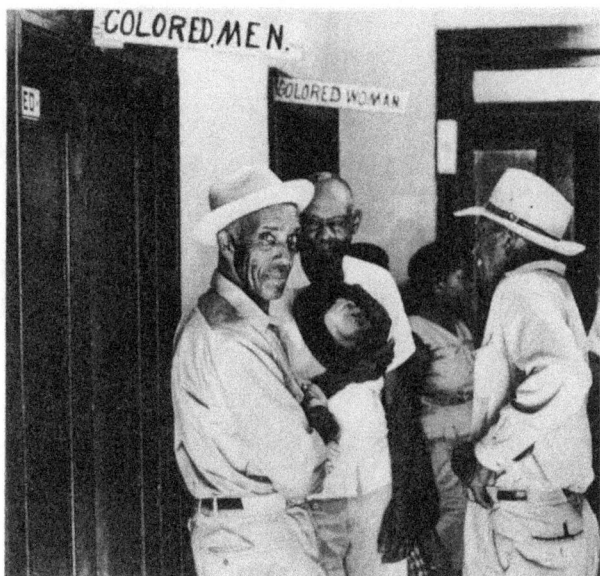

cases of rights deprivation, outside intervention was required. The League sought and received the help of the Department of Justice. The latter filed suit against the county Democratic Committee in November of 1959. In the spring of 1960, the Democratic Committee agreed to abandon the all-white primary. The whites then developed another tactic. This one was more pointed, and its opposition required more determination by the Negroes.

Fayette County does not have, so far as we know, a Ku Klux Klan chapter. But it has made abundant use of the White Citizens' Council. It was the Council that led the new attack. Blacklists were drawn up of Negroes active in the voter drive, and of whites who were sympathetic to it, as well. These lists were distributed to white merchants, farmers, and bankers, for their use in economic retaliation—for use in a boycott. Leaders of the registration drive had their names on that list marked with an "A" in the margin. "A" stood for Agitator.

Merchants refused to sell food, clothing, gasoline, and other necessities to blacklisted persons. White farmers began an explicit, publicized campaign to mechanize and convert their farms to eliminate the need for Negro labor. Negroes were evicted from the farms they had rented or worked on shares for years. Medical care, always hard to get for Negroes, became almost impossible to obtain; insurance companies canceled policies, banks called loans and withheld credit; wholesale distributors from outside the county, even, were induced not to sell to Negro storekeepers. John McFerren, leader of the League, who runs a combination grocery store and gas station, could not get gasoline for his pumps from national companies. Whether this was the result of connivance with the companies, or simply of the local police authorities stopping tank-truck drivers en route, is not yet known.

The reaction of the Negro community was twofold.

33

Registration continued, and Tent City (also called Freedom Village) was created. Tent City brought Fayette County to the attention of the nation. Tent City was a bare field which one Negro landowner turned over to those evicted from their homes for seeking their rights. In provoking this development, the whites of Fayette County aped their counterparts elsewhere; by their resistance to change, they speeded up the process and inspired new spirit and new support for the cause of civil rights in the county.

And so, the next step. The League once more appealed for help, and once again the Department of Justice took action. It filed complaints, on December 14, 1960, against forty-five landowners, twenty-four merchants, and a bank. The charge was economic intimidation, to stop Negroes from registering to vote. A few weeks later, continuing evictions were stayed by the federal district court. But "stayed" does not mean "stopped." Not until late July of 1962 was an agreement reached between Justice Department attorneys and seventy-four white businessmen and landowners, who were enjoined from engaging in any acts against Negroes who registered to vote. Even then, and down to this writing, the injunction has had more a formal than a real effect. Thus, when the Justice Department was informed in 1964 that economic intimidation continued, a Department representative responded, "The Negroes of Fayette County won a great victory in the courts; don't ask us now to rub salt in their wounds." "*Whose* wounds?" was the angry reaction of one of the Negro leaders.

National attention to the scandals in Fayette County came first in *Ebony Magazine*, in September, 1960. Later, in December, 1960, the *New York Times* ran a story about Tent City. The *Ebony* story, entitled "Cold War in Fayette County," was thoroughly researched. Not least among its useful contributions was its summation of the white point of view of what was happening, and why, in 1960. Before the registration drive of 1959, only seven tenths of one per cent of the Negroes of the county were registered. Nevertheless, in 1960, it was possible for one of the large landowners in the county to tell an *Ebony* reporter, and probably even to believe, "Niggers around here have always voted, a few anyways. Most of them just haven't been interested in politics. Only about 400 or 500 out of the 15,000 niggers around here are stirred up. The rest deplore the situation." As for economic intimidation, "There hasn't been any boycott. This is a matter of credit being withdrawn from undesirable risks. . . . " A white banker, quoted in the 1961 report of the United States Civil Rights Commission, was more candid: "My secretary's got the names of the 325 who registered. I tell them, anybody on that list, no need coming into this bank. He'll get no crop loans here. Every store has that list." And the mayor of the town was candid about one of his fears: "What we're afraid of is some unscrupulous politician getting the majority group together and upsetting the welfare of our county—electing a nigger law-enforcement officer, for example. . . . "

The Negroes of Fayette County may one day attempt to elect a Negro sheriff; in the summer of 1964 they attempted to elect a white man, L. T. Redfearn, a man they had known and trusted for more than twenty years. They also tried to elect a tax assessor, June Dowdy, a Negro minister. The character and reputation of those two men acted as one of the several elements making our summer project possible. It would not have been feasible to mount a vigorous voter registration and voting campaign had the Negroes had nobody to vote for but their oppressors. These two men had emerged as trustworthy and promising leaders in the fight that began in 1959; we met with them in Tennessee in January of 1964 to promise them that we would be in the county working for civil rights in the summer, and they gave us the assurance that they too would be fighting. But that is getting ahead of our story.

The "cold war" in Fayette County gradually became known to individuals and groups involved in the civil-rights struggle throughout the country. At one time or another, and especially in the Tent City days, SNCC, SCEF, the Quaker's Operation Freedom and others took a hand in providing food, clothing, money, and people to help those in the county. It was through these activities that students at Cornell became involved. In the summer of 1963, Walter Tillow and Charles and Rowena Haynie —respectively, graduate students in economics and mathematics and a recent graduate from Cornell—spent the summer in Fayette County helping in a voter-registration drive.

When the Haynies returned to Ithaca in September, they invited some of their friends to their home to hear of their experiences. (Tillow did not return to his studies. After the summer in Tennessee he became a full-time worker with SNCC.) It was Charlie who told the story. He had first become deeply involved in civil rights as a Mississippi Freedom Rider. Along with four other friends from Cornell, he had been sentenced to jail in Jackson, Mississippi. He had, therefore, some basis for comparison, and the story he told made Tennessee sound much like Mississippi.

As he spoke, that pleasant autumn evening, it gradually came to his listeners that he was describing a society that was lawless and impoverished and terrifying, but also a society in which hundreds of people were placing their well-being and their lives as stakes in their battle for simple dignity. Haynie spoke of the leaders, of the

36

women and children, the churches, the fields, the sheriff and his deputies (who had poured acid, for example, on one fifteen-year-old girl demonstrator that summer); he spoke of the shacks, the schools, the poverty. He told of the several beatings endured by Tillow, of the manner in which civil-rights demonstrations were manipulated by the local authorities so as to allow and encourage violence. He told us of the utter impossibility of gaining local, state, or federal protection, despite many strenuous attempts to that end.

At the end of his remarks, Charlie spoke of two men in the county, Dowdy and Redfearn, who hoped to be able to run in the county general election in August, 1964. He offered the opinion that without outside help neither man had a chance of getting out the vote, of having it rise to reasonable numbers, or of having the vote counted honestly. What was needed in the county, he thought, was a political organization, one that would take the next step beyond the League's registration campaign. But for such an organization to begin, there had to be a massive and concentrated campaign to educate the Negroes to their rights and the means of exercising them. To this end, Charlie had planned to return to the county in the summer of 1964, with a half-dozen friends. But he expected little in the way of success, given the size of the problem, given the size of the county. What was really needed, Charlie said, was a group of about twenty-five volunteers, who would spend six or eight weeks in the county; and even if one could find the volunteers, it would take about five thousand dollars to transport and support them for the summer's work.

Charlie's friends at that gathering included a few faculty members and a larger number of students—all of them seriously concerned about civil rights, some of them with a significant backlog of experience in amateur polit-

37

ical activity on and off the campus. One of these, a faculty member, pushed Charlie on his figures, and said that if that was all that was needed, a project could be organized at Cornell, easily. It could be a Cornell project, and one that would stem naturally and easily from the considerable amount of civil-rights activity and interest then existent at Cornell. Haynie now recalls that his own suggestion was quite casual, edging close to whimsy. He had nothing like an organized project in mind. But once the group present began to talk about the possibility, it became a reality. Before the evening ended, the project had a chairman and fund-raiser, a recruiter and director of volunteers and their training, and Haynie as its field director. Before long, the project had a name, a bank account, and a series of tasks to be performed. The first of these was to awaken the community to the plan, and to begin to raise money and recruit volunteers.

Chapter III

And if not you . . . ?

THE QUESTION OF CIVIL RIGHTS was not introduced at Cornell by the Fayette County Project. Like many other campuses, ours had seen a rising interest in a variety of civil-rights causes, an interest that grew steadily after the Montgomery bus strike of 1955, and especially after the student sit-ins of 1960. A few Cornell students had become deeply and personally involved, as Freedom Riders to Mississippi; there had been an active and successful Cornell Committee Against Segregation (defunct by 1964); there were scattered attempts to raise funds or clothing for SNCC projects; and so on. These were intermittent activities, however, and participation in them was limited to a handful of the same students and faculty members—limited pretty much to those, in fact, who had met to listen to Haynie when he returned from Tennessee in 1963. The Fayette Project was in part an attempt to deepen involvement and to broaden participation.

The project at Cornell quite naturally developed in terms of an appeal to the sense of social responsibility. More than that, however, the appeal focused on the responsibility of those who saw themselves as supporters of civil rights to bring their actions into line with their beliefs. It was within that framework that the theme of the project became the Talmudic injunction of Hillel: "If I am not for myself, who will be for me? And if I am for myself alone, what am I? And if not now, when?" To which there came to be added, in meetings, articles, and letters, "And if not you, who?"

In Chapter I were mentioned two critical aspects of the project making for its success, its immediacy and concrete nature, and the receptive situation in Fayette County. There was a third vital characteristic. From the beginning, our appeal was directed to the entire community, on and off campus, rather than only or even primarily to those previously caught up in civil-rights activities. This broad approach enabled us to raise more money; more important, it brought to us, and brought us to, many who had hitherto been but spectators of the movement. More than a few of these were later to become a part of the movement.

We raised more than three times the money we had initially set as a goal. More than twice the volunteers we had hoped for signed up, and more would have, had we not stopped recruiting in midspring. Scores of people helped out in important ways as the project developed. In all these respects, there were many who were as surprised as they were gratified to find themselves so much involved—as they wrote a check for twenty-five dollars or a hundred dollars, never having written a "political" check before; as they signed up to go to Tennessee, and changed their summer plans; as they argued for hours with skeptics, having perhaps but recently been skeptics themselves. The breadth of the project's appeal, in intent and in effect, will not always be made explicit as we detail the steps of its development; but that aspect of it should not to be overlooked, for it was most important.

ANNOUNCEMENT AND EARLY PLANS

The first glint of publicity for the project was a letter to the student newspaper, the *Cornell Daily Sun,* in

October, 1963. The *Sun* is a superior college newspaper, and it has a broad audience. The letter described the beginnings of our "county-to-county" civil-rights project, and the reasons for it. The letter was designed to arouse the interest of those in the community most likely to respond quickly to any such development. The response was immediate, nor was it entirely confined to people more than usually sensitive to civil-rights activities. Within a few weeks, a dozen or more people were available to lay plans for the first public meeting, to be held in December.

The meeting was to be "public" in a limited sense only. Those invited were selected in terms of that part of the university or the town they represented, actually or potentially. The meeting was quietly announced in the press, and invitations were sent to about one hundred people. Nobody was to be turned away at the door, but the intent was an organizational, not a mass, meeting.

The invitation was a four-page mimeographed document. The first page, the invitation itself, stated why the addressee had been invited. The next two pages were a statement of the problems and possibilities of Fayette County, and described the nature of the project. The last page listed all those to whom the invitation had been sent. This had the effect of letting everyone know with whom he would be meeting, and at the same time placed some pressure on each person to attend.

The percentage of those invited that came to the meeting was quite high. Addressees included the following: students in campus political organizations, regardless of political position, fraternity and sorority leaders, members of student government, representatives of men's and women's dormitories, and selected graduate students; representatives of most campus and town publications and radio stations, and of the one television station in town; selected teachers and students from grade schools, junior high, and high schools; ministers, lawyers, doctors, and businessmen of the community; faculty members of Cornell and Ithaca College, from various parts of their respective campuses.

Those who were invited were informed that they would participate in the planning of the project from the beginning, and that they would be asked to accept some degree of responsibility for it throughout. It was to be the project of this group, not of any previously existing organization. The diversity of the group's members—in age, political viewpoint, experience or lack of it, degree of commitment—proved to be of great value in planning the project. Clearly, those with experience could and did help to get things moving quickly. Those who were new to such activities brought fresh ideas to the task; they also raised questions which continued to emerge from the broad and growing audience to which we made our appeal over the ensuing months. Some of the questions seemed naive, or worse, to the "old hands." But that these questions were known early made it easier for us to come to grips with them, as they repeatedly arose from the large group whose support we sought and required.

The diversity referred to above may be suggested by a few examples. Present that first evening were both a ten-year-old boy and an emeritus professor approaching his 103rd birthday; two or three young people who believed in *any* steps that might be necessary to advance civil rights, up to and including armed intervention in the South, and also several people who were puzzled as to the need for *any* kind of intervention by "outsiders." These and other diversities made the first meeting of the group a stormy one. Significantly, however, when the meeting concluded, committees with important responsibilities had been formed, and they included people representing all the diversities present. Also, several hundred dollars had been raised on the spot, to meet oncoming expenses.

Three jobs had to be taken up immediately. First, there had to be a planning meeting in Tennessee, very soon; second, a fund-raising campaign had to be launched, whose climax would be reached in Cornell's largest auditorium, in March; third, volunteers had to be recruited and trained. The implementation of each of these will now be examined.

PLANNING MEETING IN NASHVILLE

The Fayette County Project was one of voter registration, with the connected aim of working toward a full, free, and fair election. The January meeting in Tennessee was one which would include, among others, the two candidates for office, the Rev. Dowdy and L. T. Redfearn, and we were to ask them to come to Ithaca in March. Why should that be necessary? Or was it even proper? The answers to these questions rest on a complex of reasons, combining innocence with sophistication, and distrust with confidence. Above all, for present purposes, those answers reveal some of the problems that arise when a project requiring militancy attempts to develop support from people with new, or wobbly, commitments.

We had to get to know and work with Dowdy and Redfearn and McFerren for two quite contrasting reasons —one had to do with the political imperatives of Fayette County; the other had to do with the suspicions and prejudices of people in our own community. Let us take these up in order.

Our project was not designed to elect candidates in Fayette County. But we could scarcely urge Negroes to endure the hardships and risks associated with registering and voting, only to vote for their oppressors. The Ne-

43

groes of the county had to have candidates of their own choosing on the ballot, or a "free and fair election" would be no more than a cruel joke. In fact, Dowdy and Redfearn were men who had gained the trust and respect of the county's Negroes. If there was to be a voting campaign, that had to be linked to their election campaign. And, as earlier pointed out, if they were to conduct a strong election campaign, there had to be a strong voting campaign. We had to work *with*, but not *for*, the two candidates. And that meant we had to plan with the candidates, from the beginning. For many in Ithaca, the subtleties of this problem could not be appreciated, and we were thus frequently accused of simple partisanship. Our answer finally became the weary one that civil rights and the Fifteenth Amendment are not partisan issues.

There was another reason for meeting with the candidates and McFerren (leader of the League) in January and for bringing them to Ithaca in March, and that was based on the skepticism and distrust of some of the newcomers helping in the early development of the project. Part of this was due to the mistaken notion that politics in Fayette County could be compared with politics in Tompkins County; that is, "we should see and hear the candidates." More important were negative notions arising from prejudice or stereotyped ideas of the qualifications of Negroes, especially the uneducated Negroes of Fayette County. Also, there were many who could not believe in the integrity of Redfearn, the white candidate for sheriff. Few could understand why a white Southern farmer would take the stand he did, and suffer as much as it was said he had—what was in it for him? (When he did come to Ithaca, Redfearn was asked "why?" countless times. His answer—"I don't know, I guess my daddy just raised me to be a good Christian"—was so simple as to leave the questioners still dissatisfied.) One of the in-

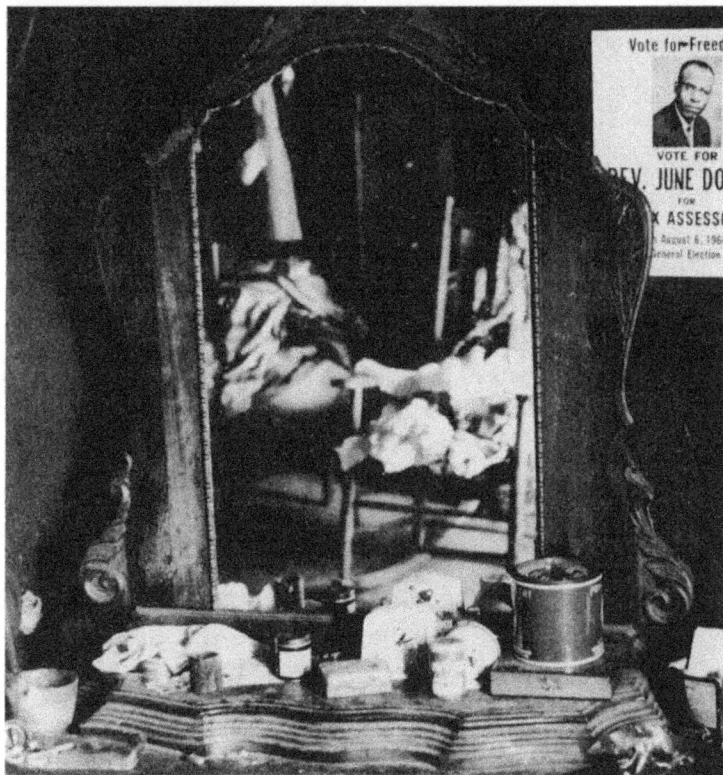

triguing aspects of this problem was that few skeptics ever raised questions concerning the ability or integrity of the incumbent whites.

When all these questions arose at our December meeting, there were many of the more experienced who were furious, and not merely from impatience. There were others, however, who saw that, after all, this project either had to be able to answer such skeptics, or it would bog down from the beginning and end up with half a dozen volunteers—back where we had started in September. Finally, the skeptics had their way; later, they were convinced.

In mid-January, about twenty people converged on Nashville for a meeting that in one form or another continued for about thirty-six hours. Those present included a reporter from the *Ithaca Journal,* the leaders of the project from Cornell, the field director of the project, some students from New York City (brought in by a Cornell graduate) who were to help raise money and volunteers, the Negro civil-rights leader of Fayette County and the two men who were to run for office, two representatives from SCEF and one from SNCC, and several people working for civil rights in Nashville, who were to help us in later stages of the project.

At that meeting, we came to know and respect each other very quickly. We put together plans for the spring and the summer bit by bit, to the degree that seemed necessary and feasible at that time. We listened to those from SNCC and SCEF as they told us of experiences in similar projects. When the meeting finally ended, everything seemed to be hanging in mid-air, but the next steps were already being taken.

The most immediate of these entailed a trip to Fayette County by the reporter, Donald Greet, who drove to the county with Dowdy, McFerren, and Redfearn. It was a momentous trip, from the project's point of view. On the flight from New York to Nashville, the reporter had made it quite clear to the project chairman that he saw the entire project through a glass darkly. He was one of the skeptics. His meeting with the three Fayette County men in Nashville had begun to change his mind. (His reaction to the Rev. Dowdy, after an evening's discussion was: "Why, he's a Goddamned folk hero!") The visit to the county itself made him one of our most valuable supporters. Greet toured the county taking pictures and asking questions, and he even had the experience of being chased—as he, a white man, drove around with Negroes known to be active in civil rights.

Upon his return to Ithaca, Greet induced his paper to run a series of five stories, with photographs, of the situation in the county. These stories were timed to build up interest and information for the March fund-raising meeting. Greet also helped to design a leaflet, of which ten thousand were printed. These were most useful in drawing the attention of potential supporters to the project. The leaflet spread about Cornell and Ithaca, and it was also sent out in hundreds to friends elsewhere. It brought back many sizable checks.

It is worth noting that Greet's paper, the *Ithaca Journal*, a member of the Gannett chain, ran his stories as part of a series on "The Road to Integration." For that series, the Gannett chain received a 1964 Pulitzer Prize, the only time a chain has been so honored. Greet later left the paper, and he has since spent most of his energies as a writer inquiring into the nature and background of the civil-rights struggle in the United States. He displayed no such bent before his involvement with the project.

The Tennessee meeting left us with plans to bring the Fayette County men up to Ithaca in March, as well as plans, from which we could not now turn back, to have a full-fledged project during the summer. It was essential that our March meeting be a success.

RAISING THE MONEY

Our big fund-raising meeting was planned for March 2, in an auditorium which holds more than two thousand people. We knew it would take much effort and imagination to fill the auditorium; how much, we did not know. We also guessed that once people came, we could succeed in getting significant contributions from them, but we did not anticipate the better than four dollars apiece they gave.

Letters to newspapers and to friends, articles, radio and television programs, interviews and other techniques were used to publicize the project and the meeting. Probably the prime means utilized in all these was the leaflet referred to earlier. It showed a picture of two Negro children standing before a shack in the hard January sunshine of Fayette County. Above the photo was the caption, "This is Fayette County, Tenn., Today . . . " Below the picture, it said, " . . . YOU Can Contribute to a Brighter Future. Bailey Hall Rally, March 2, 8 p.m." Inside the leaflet were pictures of Dowdy and Redfearn, with a brief statement of their platforms and a quotation from each. Dowdy: "I think there is an inward eagerness for this change. Some of the peoples would shout for joy." Redfearn (a white man): "Complexion has nothing to do with it. I only know one way to do business and that is fair and honest." Greet also wrote and included in the leaflet a brief background statement, "The Fayette Story," which ended, "On a county-to-county basis Tompkins' residents who have a great deal can reach out to residents of Fayette who have almost nothing—except the courage to risk everything in their belief in a better future."

A bank account in the name of the Fayette County Fund had been set up, and a post-office box taken out in the same name.* As a result of leaflet mailings, and other appeals, checks began to come in even before the meeting—from Ithaca, from San Francisco, from New Delhi, from Lagos, Nigeria. In addition to money, we received many inquiries from people who wished to join the project.

Before the meeting in Bailey Hall, about two thousand dollars had been collected. When the meeting closed, over three thousand dollars more had been given, and another two thousand dollars came in on the heels of the meeting. To obtain that sum, we spent well over a thousand dollars—transporting the Fayette County men, printing leaflets, mailing, and so on.

About seven hundred people came to the meeting. That figure may be looked at in two ways—as very small, or as very large. Only a third of the auditorium was filled, and empty seats are always a sad sight. But those seven hundred people probably included several hundred who had never attended such a meeting before, and all gave generously. In addition to what was given that night, contributions poured in through the mail in the next week or two. In one way or another, the meeting by itself brought in the five thousand dollars we sought. The meeting itself was a simple affair, with brief speeches by the three men from the county, and an appeal for funds by the project chairman, Professor Dowd. The meeting opened with civil-rights and folk songs by a talented local group calling itself the North Quarry Street Irregulars.†

* Both still exist, and contributions are still needed, for next summer's work. Send them to P. O. Box 259, Ithaca, N. Y.

† "Irregulars" because its membership has been inconstant. At the time of the meeting the trio was composed of Ruth Perry (graduate student), Rosie Stoehr (faculty wife), and George Ward (law student).

The group also sang while contributions were being made.

The technique used to gain contributions at the auditorium was most effective. Each member of the audience was given one of the leaflets as he entered; enclosed in the leaflet were blank checks from the two local banks. It is quite probable that many people who wrote checks for twenty dollars or more might otherwise have given currency in some fraction of that amount.

The folk singers, though an amateur group, are well thought of by all who have heard them. Before the meeting, we discussed the desirability and feasibility of having them cut a record, which the project would produce, and from which all proceeds would go to the Fayette County Fund. The amount of money collected by the close of the big meeting, and the fine reception given the singers, decided us. Local people with the appropriate expertise—including a high-fidelity equipment firm, and a trained engineer—contributed their services for making a tape. The tape was manufactured into a thousand long-playing records by a national firm, at conventional costs. The records cost us about $1.00 apiece, and we sold them at $3.50 apiece, netting over two thousand dollars from the record alone. Furthermore, the Irregulars performed at several concerts and smaller fund-raising meetings in New York City, Cambridge, and Buffalo, not only selling their record but gaining additional contributions. Also, they sang many times, and took collections, at the Unmuzzled Ox, a coffee and hamburger and conversation spot located in the basement of the parish house of the Lutheran Church in Ithaca's Collegetown.

As a result of having read an article about the project in the *Monthly Review*, a small group of people in New York City asked to have someone meet with them to explain the project further, and to raise funds. Don Greet (the reporter), then living in New York, and John Oliver Killens, the novelist (who had come to know McFerren in Tent City days), met with the group, and collected about $1,500—this from fewer than thirty people.

While Dowdy, McFerren, and Redfearn were in Ithaca for the meeting, we had the opportunity to develop our summer plans still further. Of equal importance, a reception was held for the three men in the Lutheran parish house. This enabled the most interested of our supporters, and not least the volunteers themselves, to meet these men. Everyone who did so gained a new understanding, by that simple act, of why such projects are necessary, and why they can succeed. A brief conversation with L. T. Redfearn was enough to convince the skeptical that here was a man with whom one could work with confidence, even if there remained some who could not fathom his character. McFerren never failed to impress those who met him with his determination, his courage, and his fine wit. The Rev. Dowdy's solid courage and blazing determination to bring about change were all the more impressive for being expressed quietly. Later, the volunteers were to discover that these men were not unusual in Fayette County—except, of course, that Redfearn's position as a white man was virtually unique.

Most of the funds, then, were raised through appeals, concerts, meetings, and record sales. But there was one source of funds that was perhaps the most important of all, in its ramifications if not in its magnitude. That was a grant of a thousand dollars made by the Executive Board of Cornell Student Government. The story of that grant, and even more, of the turmoil that followed it, is worth recounting in detail.*

* One incident concerning money should be recounted here, both because it is the sort of thing that must be expected to arise, and because it is fitting to mention the generosity of the person

One of the students invited to the December meeting was a member of the Executive Board of Student Government. He was a sensitive young man, and he had been concerned with the movement, but he had never been involved. His involvement in the Fayette County Project, which began with an invitation to a strange meeting, ultimately brought the whole campus into a conflict which was without precedent in the University's past. Finally, he decided to spend a summer in Tennessee, as did another member of the Board.

Students at Cornell, as at most other universities, have to pay fees. At Cornell, some small fraction of those fees is turned over to the Executive Board of Student Government, to disburse as it sees fit (within its constitution and bylaws) to finance recognized student activities. Student governments traditionally represent the more conservative segment of the student body, and Cornell's has been no exception. But in 1964, one of the members of the Government came to see great virtue in the Fayette County Project, and he thought that one apt use of the Board's funds would be a contribution to the project. In speaking to other members of the Board, he brought two or three over to his point of view. After the March 2 meeting at Bailey Hall, it was decided to make this a matter for formal consideration by the Executive Board. The Board has nine members, including its president. When the Board met in early March to consider this pro-

---

who helped us to resolve a crisis. During May, the bank placed irresistible pressure on Redfearn to pay two thousand dollars on a loan. Payment could be postponed if he would withdraw from the campaign. He had no way to raise such money. Nor could we in conscience use contributions for that purpose, vital though it was. Herbert Schnopper, a physicist at Cornell, came to our rescue with a personal loan to Redfearn.

posal, the president and perhaps three others were favorable to the grant. The meeting at which the proposal was considered was open to the student body, and it was attended by well over a hundred people, including some from the faculty and administration.

The meeting lasted for four hours. Had a vote been taken at the beginning, it would have been six to three against; or at best, five to four against. After an uproarious and heated four hours of debate, coming from all sides, the final vote was taken, and the proposal won, six to three. But that was only the beginning, if a surprising one.

Within minutes, one member of the Board and a student who was chairman of the campus Conservative Club (called, aptly, The Gentlemen of the Right), had determined to petition for a referendum on the Board's decision. To do so, it was required that they get the signatures of one tenth of the undergraduate student body, or about 950 signatures. In the ensuing election (which had to be held within three weeks), they had to gain two thirds of the vote to overturn the Board's decision. Within days, they had obtained about 2,300 petition signatures. Since in no election at Cornell had there ever been more than about 2,200 votes altogether, it was widely assumed that the referendum would succeed and the grant would be withdrawn. But that assumption rested on the notion that this was going to be just another campus vote. It was anything but that.

For the next three weeks, the campus was in an uproar. In the student-union building, tables were set up at which representatives of the contending points of view sat all day and much into the night. The lobby of the student union was filled with scores of students, arguing, gesticulating, planning, and sometimes threatening to come to blows. The student newspaper was utterly dominated by the issue. The editor-in-chief was a partisan of the grant; the managing editor was opposed. The editor in charge of the letters page was in favor. Some of the reporters were opposed. Articles, letters, ads in the newspaper mounted, and intensity joined with innuendo to divide the campus into two sharply discernible groups. The radio station (student-owned and operated) was against the grant. The students in charge subsequently went so far as to phone the sheriff of Fayette County and interview him on the air, concerning his "ideas" about the project. That this was a dangerous thing to do apparently did not occur to those responsible for it; they had become convinced that they were defending eternal principles.

What were the principles of those against the grant? They were not, "of course," based upon opposition to civil rights for Negroes. Nor, they said, were they opposed to the Fayette County Project. Not, at least, at first. What they were opposed to was using student fees to finance a partisan project. Their cry became "taxation without representation." So the argument turned on whether or not the Fayette County Project—a voter-registration and voting project—was partisan. That some of those opposed to the grant were opposed to civil rights too may be taken for granted—not least because some of the most vocal were themselves from the South. But there was something more substantial involved, and that was the deeper meaning of civil rights for all Americans. Hence, the long debate at the University was most educational for all concerned. One of its important by-products was to stimulate contributions to the Fund, and to induce some students to become volunteers. Most interesting among these was the editor of the paper, who wrote eloquent editorials supporting the grant and the project, and ultimately was convinced that there was only one way for *him* to answer the question he asked frequently—"If not you, who?"—and that was by spending his summer in Fayette County.

When the vote was taken, over 4,500 had voted, and over 2,500 had voted in favor of the grant. The vote against, some noted, was 1,984. Only one third of the vote had been necessary, but well over half had been gained, and that in an election which was the largest in the University's history. How and why had this happened? Here, as in all aspects of the project's history, many people became actively involved who had never been involved before. Campus elections had always been mostly inside and trivial contests; this one, it soon became evident, was not at all trivial, nor was it concerned with an "inside" issue. Hundreds of Cornell students found themselves arguing, speaking before groups, passing out handbills, and voting, who had always scorned these activities before. There were many, very simply, who could not stomach the possibility that the student body of Cornell University would go on record as opposing a civil-rights project—in whatever guise the opposition might see itself.

So, the project took in another thousand dollars; more than that, the project became a part of the lives of hundreds, perhaps thousands, of students and faculty, all of whom are now more sensitive to such questions, and considerably more alert to the nuances of arguments concerning specific civil-rights disputes.

THE VOLUNTEERS

Money, money, money; always, if something is to be done, money is required. But the money was needed to support the volunteers, and it was on the quality and the quantity of volunteers that the project depended, finally. Who were they? What led them to become volunteers? How were they chosen? How were they trained? What were they to do? What were they *not* to do?

While the fund-raising was going on, after January, the problem of the volunteers was also being worked out. Patricia Griffith was placed in charge of that vital job. Pat is the wife of Joe Griffith, a graduate student who had been a Freedom Rider with Haynie, earlier, and she is the mother of three small children. Pat knew most of the students and adults in Ithaca who had been active in civil-rights groups, and she is a person of considerable organizational ability, as well as boundless energy. The project needed all the ability and energy she could offer; in addition, it needed all the wisdom we could muster collectively, to resolve the many problems of principle and practice that inevitably arose.

From the first, those leading the project decided that we would not urge anyone to volunteer. We were aware of the dangers of the project, and it was agreed that anyone who went must have made the decision to do so in his own terms, without persuasion. As it developed, that decision not only gave us more peace of mind, it also allowed us to enroll more than enough volunteers.

All who inquired concerning the summer were put in touch with Pat, whether they had written from afar, or communicated verbally with one of us on the campus. Pat kept a record, took down all the relevant information concerning each potential volunteer, and kept in touch with all of them as the spring semester went on. By late March, more than forty had indicated strong interest; as April began, the number rose to fifty. Ultimately, more than sixty had made serious inquiries. Most were students at Cornell, undergraduate and graduate. A few were ex-Cornellians who learned of the project from friends. Some were friends of Cornell students at other campuses. How to choose from among them?

Charlie Haynie, the field director of the project, had by March decided that we needed a minimum of thirty volunteers, and could use a maximum of forty-five. The county is divided into fifteen election districts, and the plan of the project was to have one twosome in each district. The "extra" fifteen would be used for special purposes, mostly in the election districts so large as to require more than two people. Because each volunteer had to be housed with a Negro family in the county,* there could not be more than about forty; for it was an act of substantial courage, and some sacrifice, for the Negro families to house civil-rights workers. How to choose?

We decided quite soon that whatever selection process was used, it would not be based upon the decisions of the leadership, but essentially upon the decisions of the volunteers themselves. That is, the volunteers were to weed themselves out, and to do so through their participation in, and reactions to, a two-month series of training sessions. We assumed, and correctly, that those who would be most likely to work out in the project would be those who found themselves most in accord with the nature and purposes of the group as these developed in the training sessions.

"Training session" is perhaps too fancy a term for the meetings of the volunteers that went on through April and May. The group met in a room on campus once a week, on Sunday afternoons, for two months. The first few meetings were taken up with general discussions of what we were trying to accomplish, the proposed means of accomplishment, and a few general rules. It was

* Charlie asked some of the people in the county what would be a reasonable amount to pay for the food of each volunteer, since we would be eating and sleeping in the homes of people who could barely support themselves, let alone guests. We paid twice the suggested amount, to make sure that we would not add to the hardships of our hosts.

agreed that we would have few rules, that we would come to agreement upon what those should be by general discussion, and that once agreement was reached it would be binding upon all. Those who still disagreed could, as some did, leave the project. Any who broke a rule during the summer could be ordered to leave the county.

Quite naturally, one of the very first and most persistent questions to arise had to do with violence, weapons, and behavior with respect to intimidation and threats. The group was at first seriously divided on the question of weapons, some thinking it only sensible that we be armed, others thinking very much the opposite. The chairman of the project was adamantly opposed to the carrying of weapons by any volunteer, and he used his position to argue forcefully to that end. After considerable discussion pro and con a consensus emerged: The safest thing we could do was to remain completely unarmed, for any weapons would furnish a pretext to attack us (in "self-defense"); anyhow, few of us knew how to handle weapons effectively or safely. The discussion on this matter was heated; but once the decision was reached, everyone agreed to be bound by it.*

It was also decided that if someone was attacked, he should decide for himself whether to respond nonviolently or in kind. The project was not, in principle, one of nonviolent resistance. More will be said later of what in fact happened in this respect during the summer; suffice it to say, now, that nonviolent resistance was the response of everyone attacked, regardless of principle. The reason for this was simple; nobody was ever attacked unless outnumbered by the attackers.

Other general rules were adopted in the sessions. First,

* In this, as in other instances, there were some violations of rules during the summer, as will be shown in the next chapter.

it was agreed that in the county there would be one rule, and that was the field director's. Everything could be discussed and argued—and was, endlessly—but once a decision was made, Haynie's word was to be law. Second, because Fayette County is a dry county, a rule against drinking of any kind was adopted. This was agreed to principally because anyone found in possession of spirits could be arrested on the spot, and thereby cause trouble for the entire project.

Then there was the problem of sex. Some of our volunteers were married couples, and they would work and live together. No problem there. It is of course a commonplace among Southern whites that civil-rights workers are sexual deviates at worst, sexually promiscuous at best. We wished to add no fuel to those particular fires, but neither did we propose to go out of our way to change the minds of these Southerners, it being assumed that nothing we might do or not do would convince them. We were, however, concerned that the Negroes of the county not look upon the volunteers as morally defective; for it was our understanding that the morality of that religious county was quite strict. Consequently, we set a few interconnected rules concerning discretion in behavior, speech, and dress. Those rules were generally followed, but for reasons more connected with the character of the volunteers than with any compulsion from the environment. We found that the people of the county thought so highly of our presence and our intentions that our personal behavior and idiosyncrasies were of no interest to them. In the event, celibacy or its opposite was a problem neither of principle nor of practice. There was, however, a serious incident concerned with drinking, and that will be discussed in context.

The training sessions had one other problem that Pat tried to solve. Here was a fairly large group of Ivy-

League students preparing to spend six to eight weeks in the rural South. They would be living and working with impoverished Negroes whose whole life experience had been confined to agriculture, largely devoid of the intellectual and cultural backgrounds of the volunteers. We had to learn as much as possible about the life and work and attitudes of our hosts, and of the county, in order to minimize mistakes and offensive behavior. There was also the simple problem of health.

Toward a solution of these questions, Pat organized a series of sessions with outside speakers, ranging from two ministers with substantial experience in the rural South, to an agronomist and a sociologist whose backgrounds and much of whose work involved the South; there were talks by Haynie, based upon his own experiences in the county in 1963, and a detailed discussion by an informed doctor of health, sanitation, and disease as relevant to Fayette County. The volunteers, in retrospect, found many of these sessions useful, and some of them not so. One session in particular, though it had no practical relevance for some of the volunteers, served to bolster their confidence at the same time that it scared some of them; it was a session in the techniques of nonviolent resistance, given by an experienced civil-rights worker.

The sessions served one important additional function. They enabled the volunteers to get to know each other, and ultimately to become paired off in a more or less natural way. Thus, by the end of May, Pat and Charlie had a pretty fair idea of who should work with whom, who should drive to the county with whom, and so on. The transportation arrangements were themselves something of a tangle at first, for the group went down in small groups rather than all at once. But that was worked out without undue strain.

As a consequence of the doctor's session, all the volunteers were required to take shots at the campus clinic, for tetanus, typhoid, poliomyelitis, and infectious hepatitis. For further security, the members of the project were insured through a policy available (surprisingly) to groups such as our own, by the Brotherhood Mutual Life Insurance Company of Fort Wayne, Indiana. All volunteers were insured for a very small sum against sickness, accident, dismemberment, or death from the time they left Cornell until they arrived back home. The amount paid to the company came to something over two hundred dollars; the amount received back from the company for claims came to a little under two hundred dollars. The company was most gracious, co-operative, and prompt.

One further precaution was taken in the spring. We hired a Tennessee lawyer. This was done through an ex-Cornellian resident in Nashville. A retaining fee of a thousand dollars was required, with the provision that another five hundred dollars would be paid if the lawyer found himself much involved. He did, and the fee had to be paid.

Many of the volunteers were under twenty-one years of age, and there was some reason for their parents to be worried. Where possible, parents were contacted, through the mails or in visits. What reassurance could be given was given. In one case, a volunteer was induced—not required—to withdraw because of serious parental concern.

By the time May had ended, Haynie was already in Fayette County, finding places for the volunteers to live, and beginning to lay the groundwork for their political activity in the county. The volunteers had selected themselves. How did such a selection process work out during the summer? We discovered that any criteria we might have used for weeding people out would have been wrong. Those who seemed too shy turned out to be determined and vigorous workers. Those who seemed too brash were softened. In one way or another, those who went were made by the context into the kind of people they had to be. That is another lesson we learned.

Now, let us study the context—the summer.

Chapter IV

The summer's work

As soon as classes were over in early June, groups of volunteers set off for Fayette County in the old cars—some donated by well-wishers, some personal property—which were to be a constant, but essential, headache. By the end of June all the permanent members of the project were settled in Negro homes and busily canvassing the fifteen election districts of the county.

The induction ritual was always the same. A fresh carload of volunteers would drive up to McFerren's store, an incongruously bright brick-and-concrete fortress perched on the edge of Somerville. Lounging near the gas pumps would be a few elderly Negroes with no place to go, some tough-looking kids drinking coke—and whatever volunteers had come to headquarters for mail, gas, car repairs, or counsel. While the new arrivals took in the rock-and-roll music blaring from the nearby cafe, the grinning veterans passed on the latest news of arrests or violence.

Then Charlie Haynie would emerge from the little shack that served as the office of the Original Fayette County Civic and Welfare League and take the newcomers in hand. Sometimes the news was good: "You'll be staying with the Williamses in District 7. The district is well-registered, with a helpful leader. I'll take you out now and get you settled." Other times it was not so simple: "We couldn't find a place for you in this district, but there's a mass meeting in one of the churches tonight, so we'll just stand up at the end and ask someone to give you a bed."

Accommodations varied from bearable to comfortable. Most volunteers found themselves in flimsy frame houses without plumbing, sharing a bed with a partner (of the same sex). The few who landed in the homes of more prosperous Negroes might have a shower. Host families received a meager five dollars per week from the project for boarding and feeding a volunteer. Though five dollars was often equal to the weekly cash income of a Fayette County Negro (a maid receives no more than $1.50 for a day's work), the risk of losing a job or the fear of trouble made homes difficult to find.

Certain features of daily life in the county were a fixed background to the project's activities. An excerpt from one project worker's diary expresses the timeless feeling of the rural South:

Up at 6:30 as usual and Mrs. C. had breakfast waiting: biscuits, eggs, fresh sausage, instant coffee—all greasy. Got a bucket of water from the pump and helped Mrs. C. do the dishes. All the rest of the family out chopping cotton. Then set out to fill in back roads that we missed on our first sweep through the district. Today we'll have Jim, a bright fifteen-year-old who doesn't seem to have any job, riding with us as guide.

In the first month, the volunteers' effort was a two-pronged one: to compile as accurate a list of registered persons and potential registrants as possible; and to persuade the unregistered to go down to the courthouse themselves, or to provide them with transportation to the courthouse on the next Wednesday. The registration drive was of prime importance until Wednesday, July 1, when by Tennessee law the books were closed in preparation for the county general election and state primary on August 6.

Project members were soon welcome, if never quite at home, in the county. Very quickly the Negroes of the county showed us they felt that we were not run-of-the-mill white folks (three of us were not white, incidentally), but new friends from outside whom they could trust. But to trust us was one matter, to place their own lives and well-being in extra jeopardy by registration was, for many, quite another. At first new registrants were somewhat less than easy to persuade; the whole project was strange, and the memory of the costs to previous registrants was still fresh. Our progress took place in a steplike, rather than a straight-line, fashion. That it would be so was seen early by one of our new friends, a minister, as underscored by a story he told. This story, like many others circulating in the county, had more than a little wisdom in it:

There was a preacher who asked his congregation, "How many of you want to go to heaven? Raise your hand." One fellow didn't raise his hand. When the preacher asked, "Don't you want to go to heaven?" the man said, in a worried tone, "Yes, suh, I wants to go to heaven, all right, but not in the first load!"

The minister telling the story went on to say that almost all the Negroes in the county wanted to register, but not in the first load. The "first load" soon registered, and at the end the loads carried more hopeful registrants than we could handle.

By the last two Wednesdays before July 1, there were several hundred Negroes lined up in front of the courthouse by noon to register. Despite the age and feebleness of the single Fayette County registrar, who put on a dumb show that entailed at least fifteen minutes to write one Negro's name on a card, over fifty managed to register on each occasion. By 10:00 a.m. on Wednesday,

July 1, over four hundred Negroes were waiting in the blazing heat of the courthouse lawn to register.

This was to be our first showdown with the white authorities in Somerville. Tennessee election law provides for the closing of registration thirty days before an election; it also states that provision must be made to enable all persons who wish to register to do so. At 4:00 p.m. a record number of Negroes had managed to get through—seventy-one new registrations and forty-two changes of address, or 113 potential votes—which left more than three hundred waiting. The registrar pulled his shades, locked his office door, and drove off, probably humming quietly to himself.

Charlie Haynie's reaction was characteristic of the project approach: always give the proper authorities a chance to do what they ought to do. Thursday morning several carloads of Negroes who had tried to register the day before drove in to Memphis to the FBI. The FBI officials were brusque but not unpleasant to the student volunteers when they requested intervention to keep the registration books open. The FBI agents insisted on interviewing in private each of the slightly awed Fayette County Negroes who had volunteered to give up a day to testify. As they emerged from these interviews, the witnesses were relieved, but puzzled. "He just wrote down my name and age," said one elderly lady, "and told me we all had a lot of colored people reddished [i.e., registered] in Fayette County."

One hopes that the FBI's true position is no longer expressed by the decor of their Memphis office, where a sign reading "Impeach Earl Warren" was once posted conspicuously beside the ten most-wanted men. In any case, no action was taken, and the books remained closed. In the pressure of other activities, the volunteers had little time for frustration. The first encounter with bureaucratic indifference had two salutary effects. Even the volunteers who expected the least lost their minimal faith in the good intentions of the federal authorities and drew together; and the Negroes who had stuck their necks out for the first time on July 1 when they stood all day in front of the citadel of white authority, found their necks permanently extended. As one seventy-year-old grandmother put it, "I never reddished cause I was scared of trouble. Now I guess I know what John McFerren and them went through back in '59. They can't turn me back now. When's the next day we can reddish?"

With no more hope of registering additional Negro voters before August 6, the volunteers turned to the organization and education of those already registered. The first canvass of each district had failed to produce anything close to the figure of 4,700 registered Negroes reported by the Justice Department. Many who had responded to McFerren's call to register in 1959 and 1960 had failed to vote or re-register once in four years (as was required by law), and some told volunteers that they thought having the pink card was sufficient. As district after district reported on its canvassing, it became clear that we were dealing with 3,500 voters at most, and probably closer to 2,500. The figure the Justice Department official had given for *white* registration in Fayette County was just 3,500. It was all the more imperative, then, that every Negro who could vote be at the polls on August 6 and that his vote be counted!

The heat of June wore into the relentless humidity of July. The election loomed in the distance. From the very beginning, the teams had worked independently, feeling their way in each district. The districts varied widely, from Number 10, on the Mississippi border, with its ranks of illiterate voters and three strong, intelligent leaders, to Number 8, in the center of the county, with

many independent farmers (some of whom had voted before), and with a pocket of relatively prosperous bootleggers who found they could work well with incumbent authorities in the county and in neighboring Mississippi.

Gradually, however, a pattern emerged. During the day, when most Negroes were in the field, volunteers made plans for mass meetings or visited with leaders of districts, sections, and roads. These leaders formed the organization (analogous to the block-ward-borough structure of a city political machine) which evolved to meet the needs of communication. Literally hundreds of miles of dirt roads crisscrossed each district; it might take days to contact each of the registered Negroes individually. (One volunteer clocked 8,100 miles on his car, for the summer.) But Fayette County has a marvelous if informal communications system, as volunteers learned to their occasional dismay; one family might grumble that the "freedom riders" (as some called us) had visited their neighbors two miles away the day before and hadn't stopped by to see them. By dividing each district into five to ten sections it was possible to spread news of a meeting to several hundred persons by simply calling on each of the leaders.

The days, then, were spent in driving and talking. Both took their toll. The dirt roads and heavy use wreaked every conceivable damage on new and old cars alike. A flat tire was at least a weekly event for each car; some cars had several flats a week. The devoted mechanic at McFerren's store prescribed wheel-alignment jobs like sugar pills. Car repairs consumed far more than their allotted share of the project budget. During the several hours that volunteers were forced to spend at McFerren's waiting for their car to be fixed, they could relax, play a game of chess, write a letter on the typewriter at the Civic and Welfare League office, mimeograph a handout,

or work on their cars themselves, the "line" being so long.

Volunteers were less vulnerable than automobiles, but fourteen hours a day of speaking what someone called a foreign language strained even the calmest tempers. Despite preparations for everything from snake bites to blood blisters, no volunteers suffered any illness more serious than those known to travelers in Paris. One grew used to the lack of showers or privacy, and almost forgot about the casual drinking and sexuality of Northern student life, for every gesture in a closed society takes on enormous implications.

It was harder to realize that one was drawling and "y'alling" like a native while still having to ask the "natives" to repeat themselves again and again. Conversation in Fayette County consists of long silences punctuated by rapidly mumbled comments. In a half-hour conversation on a sharecropper's porch we might analyze the weather, the cotton crop, and the children, and then briefly talk about voting. The volunteers would discuss voting, marking the ballot, and the place to vote, and then invite the hosts to a mass meeting at a nearby church.

Rarely does the Fayette County Negro—with the exception of a few of the brash teenagers—question a white visitor. Those who were closest to the volunteers, the host families and their neighbors, were curious about many things: clothes, boyfriends or girlfriends of the unmarried volunteers (the median age of girls at marriage is about eighteen in Fayette County), their religion ("Is it true that Jews can only get married to other Jews?"), even the schools up North. But the quips and ironies of the volunteers' conversation with each other were as foreign to the Fayette County resident as his slow, needling humor was to us.

Of course, the differences in age and experience of the

Northern college students and the middle-aged Southern farmers they dealt with would be expected to present barriers to communication. The most obvious barrier, the difference in color, might be forgotten by the volunteers, but it was too important to be forgotten by the Negroes of Fayette County. Every volunteer was aware at some time that he was being "yessired" by a man twice his age, and felt a stab of shame; every volunteer had to face the fact that he could not erase in a week or a year the traditional "Mister Bob" or "Miss Judy" used in addressing white folks. What rankled in most volunteers' minds was the nagging thought that they might be using their color as a bludgeon to make Negroes register and vote.

Floyd Franklin, son of the Negro storekeeper who was heralded in the white newspaper, the *Fayette Falcon*, for supporting Sheriff Pattat, summed up the positive value of a white face when he stood up to speak at a mass meeting in one of the Negro churches, after a fiery speech by Charlie Haynie denouncing Franklin's father:

Mr. Haynie, you and your group are doing fine work. Lord knows I've worked to get people to register and vote. But you've succeeded where I've failed. And let me tell you why. Your face is white. People will listen to you. You're a man who enjoys freedom and so you can bring this idea to the people. I'm colored and not free. That is why they won't listen to me.

If the white strangeness of the volunteers worked to their advantage in the Negro community, their high visibility only made for jangled nerves in confronting—or trying to avoid—the white people of Fayette County. The project's encounters with whites were sporadic and often unpredictable. L. T. Redfearn gave us some insight into the character of the rural white Southerner, for he is Fayette County born and bred, and his own brother worked against him in the county election. But Redfearn is an articulate man and above all a decent one, a completely "Southern boy" who happened to listen to his daddy's words about treating all men as equals and took them literally. It was hard to reconcile this with the groups of pasty-faced teenagers standing by the gas pumps in small towns like Macon and Oakland and shouting "nigger lover" at the volunteers' cars as they passed.

These whites did some violence to members of the project, but not as much as there might have been, had not the wondrous grapevine of the Fayette County Negroes, with its inextricable tangle of rumor and fact, tutored us all to a fine wariness. There were only a few incidents of real and attempted mayhem, considering the number of volunteers, the time of their stay, and the purpose of the project. These incidents occurred almost entirely in the early part of the summer. More than one car was run off the road; another had a half-filled coke bottle thrown with full force into its windshield. Volunteers' cars were twice shot at (once on election day). There were three or four beatings, with the ever-present ratio of four or five to one against us that made one wonder where the notion ever began that the Southern white is the bravest of Americans. Cars were often chased and not caught, leaving the suspicion that our "escape" was due less to our skill at outracing the county's hoodlums, than to the probability that they were just trying to scare us.

There were several arrests, for trumped-up traffic violations, for carrying a gun, and most important, for trespassing. In the last-named instance, had the charge of trespassing held up the project could have been critically damaged, for much of its work had to be done on the lands of sharecroppers. A high bail (seven hundred dollars) had to be posted for the "trespassers"; subsequently we won an important victory when our lawyer forced the prosecuting attorney to concede that Tennessee law did not place our activities under the definitions of trespassing. The project breathed a collective sigh of relief.

A by-product of one of the beatings sheds some light on the notion that what is meant by success or failure for civil-rights projects must be defined carefully. Violence in the South is endemic. Moreover, the knowledge concerning who does what to whom soon becomes common to all concerned. It is quite another thing to have such knowledge transformed into evidence that will hold up in court. Two of our volunteers were set upon in ambush by four or five cars one evening, as they returned "home." Some of the cars left before the action as their occupants' courage apparently drained away. Two cars remained, and seven or eight white hoodlums set upon the project car (whose doors were locked and windows rolled up), tore the handle from one of the car doors, slashed a tire, broke windows, got one door open and managed to get a few cracks at one of the volunteers. All this happened in June. On August 7 (the day after the lost election), two young Negroes came to us to say they knew who had done the beatings, by name, by car, by license plate, and so on. They had known all the facts since the day after the event, as they heard the whites talking about it around a gas station in the area. (When asked why the whites provide them with such dangerous information, one of the Negroes replied, "They don't figure it makes much difference what we know, 'cause they know we ain't going to say anything." To which the other added, "They think it impresses us.") They knew the facts, and the hoodlums knew that they knew the facts. By August, the Negro boys (they were both aged seventeen) had been affected by the project to the point where they came forth to say they wished to report all the facts to

75

the FBI. They did so; and that was a small revolution for Fayette County. (It is also important to note that to date we have no information concerning any prosecution of the attackers, despite positive identification.)

Violence in the South did not begin with violence against civil-rights workers, of course. Negroes have suffered violence of the most depraved kinds from time immemorial. Not least among such acts has been the act of rape, of Negro women by white men. What is called rape in the North is called rape in the South, too, by the Negroes; to whites it has seemed merely another means of exploiting the Negroes. That situation may be changing now, in Fayette County. In the last two weeks of the project, a young woman was raped by a white man (thirty-five years old, father of three). She was taken at the point of a gun to the man's house in Mississippi, a few miles away, and raped while her infant daughter was in the room, and her younger sister waited outside. She had been helpful in one of our court cases a month or so before. After the rape, she was told to get going, that the house was surrounded, and that if she said anything she'd get the same treatment as those three civil-rights workers in Neshoba County. A few days later, the young woman decided she wanted to tell the FBI. Some of us went to see the FBI, and the next day they went out to the county to take the story of the young woman. The man had earlier been arrested by the Mississippi State Police and released. Whether the FBI ever acted— under the Mann Act, the Civil Rights Act of 1964, or at all—we don't know. Still, it was another small revolution; to our knowledge rapes had not been reported before, or if so, not acted upon.

It is worth recounting in detail the one really frightening threat of the summer and the way this was handled. One night in July, Maggie Mae Horton, one of the most important leaders of District 10, appeared at McFerren's store with her husband and the three white volunteers working in the district. She told Charlie Haynie and John McFerren that her son had learned that a certain white landowner had offered a Negro sharecropper five hundred dollars and a gun if he would kill Bob (but not Bob's wife Vicki, who was with him), Ron, and John, along with Herbert Bonner, a Negro from the District who was actively working with the project. Other volunteers were at the store at the time, and there were many conflicting schemes for blocking the sharecropper, tricking the landowner, or removing the four potential victims to safety. But the final decision was Charlie's. He telephoned Sheriff Pattat and demanded that he enforce the laws of the county, he called the FBI office in Memphis to report the incident, and he kept the threatened volunteers out of their district for the night. The next day the sheriff paid a call on his friend the white landowner, and the FBI came out to investigate.

No, this was not complete justice. But the volunteers got back to work the next day, and the imminent danger was averted. The more diffuse, generalized danger was always with us. With that, one learned to live, as soldiers learn to live with the sounds of gunfire, always taking the necessary precautions. In the case of the project workers, these precautions were fairly simple, if confining: never go anywhere alone, avoid driving late at night, stay off the main roads frequented by whites, lock the car doors and roll up the windows, copy down license plate numbers of ominous-appearing cars. Driving home at night from mass meetings in the Negro churches, volunteers were often followed, but it was easy enough to shake off a carload of whites looking for excitement by turning off onto one of the dirt roads where Negroes live.

And then there were a few odd encounters with the

white residents of Fayette County. One team of volunteers had a blowout on the way to Memphis, right in front of a small radio-repair shop. A white lady came out of the store and offered to lend the volunteers her jack. Sometimes, early in the summer, volunteers would mistakenly approach a house inhabited by whites (usually it is very easy to tell a white house from a Negro one—one just checks for an outhouse) and be forced to carry on as if nothing had happened: "We were just taking a survey to find out how many people are registered. You're not? Well, be sure you all go down to the courthouse and register, all right?"

Hardest of all to comprehend, however, was the attitude of the sheriff and his deputies. Again and again we heard the confounding Southern story: "Now Sheriff Pattat, he ain't a bad man. But that deputy, he's a mean one. He'd just as soon spit on you as call you by your name." As the summer progressed, Sheriff Pattat responded, albeit grudgingly, to demands for protection of the Northern agitators who had invaded his county. The previous summer, just after a group of high-school students made a disastrous attempt to integrate the movie house in Somerville, Pattat had appointed two Negro deputies to keep order in the Negro community. In the summer of 1964, Sheriff Pattat, who had campaigned in 1962 on a platform of rejecting Negro votes, suddenly changed his tune. Apparently the rumor circulating among the Negroes that Redfearn was going to win this time by a margin of seven hundred votes had reached the Sheriff's office too; in any case, with the election three weeks away Pattat was out shaking Negro hands (registered or not!) and handing out his little white cards.

Besides the sheriff and his chief deputy, the other members of the Fayette County élite were the head of the Democratic Party, who was uniformly cool and sarcastic, and the Judge. Judge Somers is one son that Yale Law School has little reason to be proud of, but even he was not completely blind to justice, when the pressure was on. In the case of *Naden v. the State of Tennessee*, for example, in which a project worker who was a law student proved he had been arrested with no grounds on a charge of reckless driving, the judge listened with a faint glimmer of amusement to the student's defense; then he reduced the charge to "failure to yield right of way."

Our encounters with whites were always rare, and divorced from the primary task of talking with Negroes. It was vital that we gain the trust of the Negro people, who have seen Northern student "work projects" come and go, along with a trickle of white visitors eager to see one of the ugliest sides of our society. It would have been impossible to win their trust if we had attempted the kind of dialogue with the Fayette County whites urged by some of our well-wishers at Cornell.

And so, through the month of July, volunteers concentrated on developing a viable political organization, on finding and training reliable, literate pollwatchers, and convincing the Negro voters to stand together. The latter motif was stated and restated a hundred different ways at church services, in freedom schools, in private conversations—and above all at the mass meetings.

A "mass meeting" might be attended by anywhere from fifty to five hundred persons, but the formula for such social-political gatherings did not vary. On Sunday it would be announced in every church in a certain area that all were invited to a mass meeting next Tuesday night at Pleasant Grove, or Oakland, or Mt. Olive, or Travelers' Rest. In their house-to-house canvassing the particular group of volunteers who were organizing the meeting would be sure to remind each family to come.

79

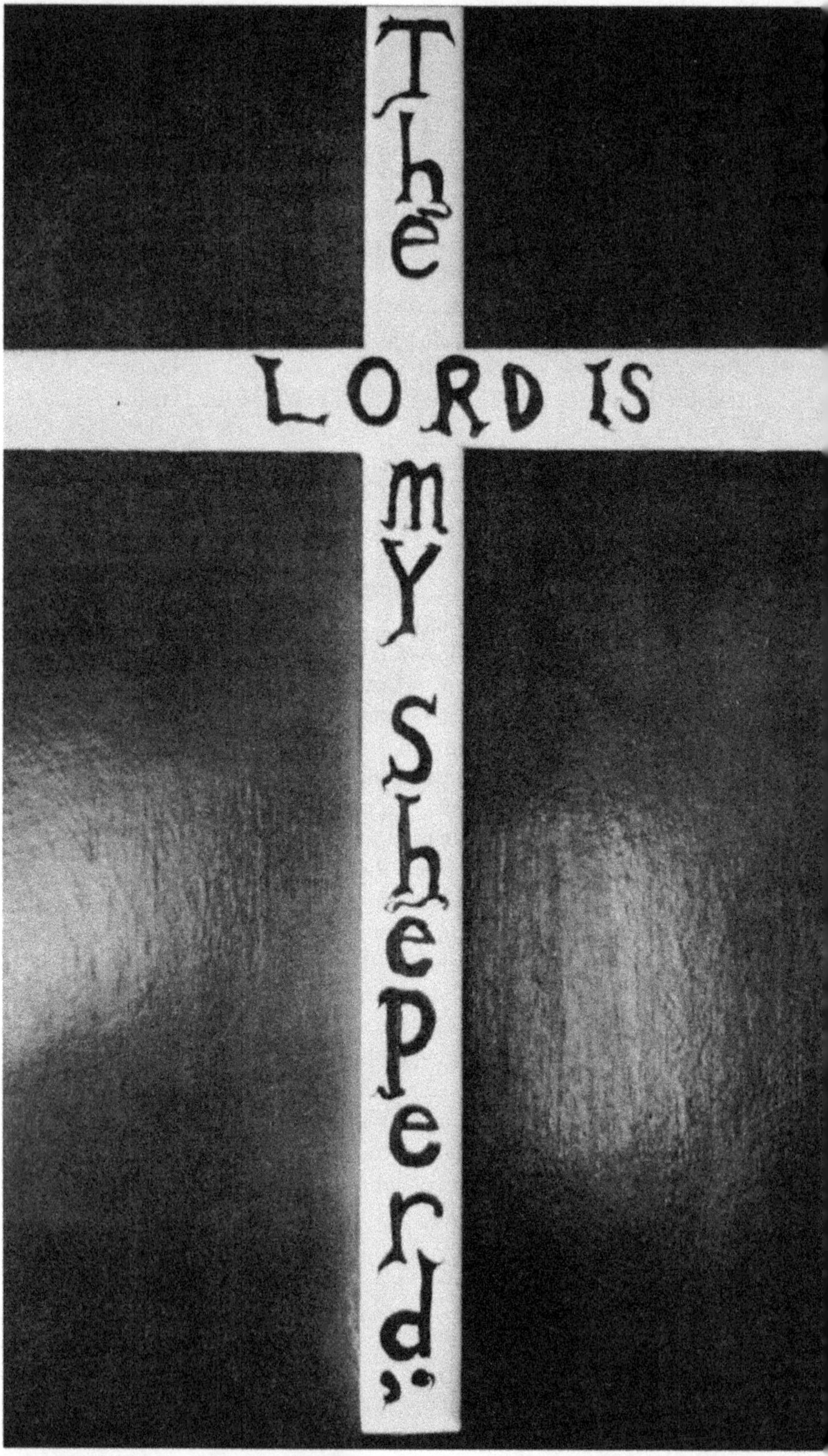
The
LORD IS
mY
Shepherd;

If the meeting had been scheduled for 8:00 p.m., the first cars full of people dressed in their Sunday best (which for men, women, and children is stylish and painfully clean in the midst of the all-pervading Fayette County dust) would begin to arrive at a quarter to nine. A conference between the volunteers and the minister of the church would decide that the meeting must start in fifteen minutes no matter what.

Meetings began with a prayer, a long chant if the church was a Baptist one, and a hymn. The body of the meeting would be organized around a particular theme—going over the sample ballot, or holding a mock election, or toward the end of July, simply the theme of solidarity. Every white visitor present would be expected to say a few words; we soon became adept at taking a small verse from the Bible or making up a simple parable and using this to talk to the people about voting.

Dowdy and Redfearn attended as many of these mass meetings as they could, which occasionally meant speaking twice or even three times a night. When the candidates were present, the meetings were particularly exciting. Both are excellent speakers. We never found out what kind of speakers their opponents, C. E. Pattat and Malcolm (Booty) Jordan, were because they never responded to an invitation to speak at one of these rallies.

The Rev. Dowdy does not belong to the tradition of ranting Southern preachers. He is so soft-spoken that an audience would often have to strain to catch his words. But strain they did, and they responded warmly to his dry humor and steadfast honesty: "They say that I don't have the education to be a tax assessor. Well, I never heard that Booty Jordan had *any*. But I am studying now to become a tax assessor and if I am elected I will work hard to find out everything there is to know about tax assessing and to treat everyone, white and Negro, fair."

Exhausted after a long day of chopping cotton and tending to his own churches, struggling to support a huge family, the very fact that Dowdy could stand up and run for office was impressive.

Redfearn, on the other hand, is a fiery orator who knows how to keep an audience in the palm of his hand. His speech was almost invariably the same, but people would go miles to a meeting to hear him again. Speaking in a relaxed, off-the-cuff manner, he reminded them of the beginning of the civil-rights struggle in 1959, when with John McFerren and others he had signed the petition that led to an injunction against seventy-three white landowners for interfering with Negroes registering and voting. "You know I was as bad off, worse maybe, than you all. I couldn't even buy a bottle of pop in Somerville. And now the Sheriff comes around and says to you, 'I done the best I could.' But you and I know that ain't nothing but a sugar tit you give to a baby to stop it from crying. Ladies and gentlemen, he's trying to give you a *pacifier*."

Both candidates grew more confident as the election drew close. Dowdy would have to win every Negro vote to be elected, but Redfearn was well known in both the Negro and white communities and had been told by his own grapevine that he could count on a sizable white protest vote. In the last few weeks before the election the mass meetings—and there were several each night in various parts of the county—took on the air of family picnics.

Not that anyone believed that either candidate would win without trouble at the polls and determination on the part of the voters. Redfearn, after all, had been through this twice before in the elections of 1959 and 1961. And less partial visitors from outside who dropped in and who talked with all segments of the population gave a more balanced and sobering view than volunteers might have seen for themselves, isolated as they were within the Negro community.

The visitors were the reporters and photographers who trooped in and out of Fayette County throughout the summer. Mississippi was the big news of the summer of 1964, of course; but a number of reporters managed to stop off in Fayette County, either on their own initiative or in response to the letters of members and friends of the project to home-town papers about the events in Tennessee. Press coverage ranged from the dispassionate rundown by David Halberstam in the *New York Times* to the somewhat warmer series written by project member Richard Denenberg for the *Herald Tribune* and the *Nation.*

Fayette County was big news for the two Memphis papers, both of which took a highly skeptical view of the Northern civil-rights workers. Among the other organs which covered the county this summer were the *Nashville Observer, Look* magazine, the *National Observer, Jet,* and *Muhammad Speaks.* NBC used several minutes of footage with Sander Vanocur on its *Huntley–Brinkley Reports.* In the last week before the election it was not uncommon to see a photographer from *Look* jostling a reporter from *Jet* at one of the small tables in the back of McFerren's grocery. McFerren assumed that all whites, other than the project workers and Redfearn, were spies.

The project itself was not the big story, of course. What brought reporters was the apparently good chance that for the first time a Negro and a white man who had worked for Negro rights might be elected to office in Black Belt country. And, their curiosity piqued by Redfearn's ebullience or McFerren's good-humored belligerence, many stayed on for election day.

Election day began at 6 a.m. for volunteers and poll-watchers. The pollwatchers, three for each polling place, were armed with copies of the Tennessee election manual and a certificate saying "I appoint _____ as my official pollwatcher in District _____." These were signed by Dowdy, Redfearn, or Ross Bass, who was seeking the Democratic senatorial nomination. We had learned the day before from Joe Cocke, the head of the Fayette County Democratic Party and also the Commissioner of Elections, that Redfearn's pollwatchers would be denied admittance to the polls. Since Redfearn was running as an independent candidate, said Cocke, he was not covered by the legal provision for a pollwatcher for the candidate of each party. Therefore, a trained poll-watcher went to each polling place armed with a certificate signed by Redfearn and an affidavit, which he was prepared to sign immediately after being turned away.

The Redfearn and Dowdy pollwatchers were, in fact, turned away at all but two polling places, where the officials seemed not to have gotten the word from Mr. Cocke. But the pollwatchers bearing certificates signed by Ross Bass, pro-civil-rights candidate for the Democratic senatorial nomination (to fill the seat vacated by the death of Estes Kefauver) had better luck. In all but two districts, the Ross Bass pollwatchers were admitted with little or no fuss and allowed to observe almost all of the election.

Ross Bass allowed his appeal for the Democratic nomination in Fayette County to be based on the fact that his two opponents, Governor Clement and Frank Bullard, were competing for the segregationist vote. Bass never campaigned personally in Fayette County; nevertheless, his stated appeal for Negro votes and the fact that he allowed his pollwatching certificates to be distributed by the Fayette County Project insured him the Negroes' votes.

Despite weeks of training in all the minor provisions of Tennessee election law, it required great courage for a Fayette County Negro to stand all day in a room with fourteen white election officials—the most powerful whites in his neighborhood—and try to write down and object to any violation. The men and women who managed to get into the polling places behaved superbly, although they were unable to stop cheating by the election official or to guard against the trickery that occurred between the time the polls closed and the counting began. Nevertheless, their very presence was heartening to the Negro voters and a symbol of the new Negro strength in the eyes of the white officialdom.

After attempting to place pollwatchers in each voting place, the volunteers retreated from public view. The weeks of small meetings of "roads" and "sections" paid off on election day. The usual confusion of people waiting for a ride to the polls and never making it, while other cars went half empty, gave way to an efficient transportation system by which every registered person was provided with a ride to and from the polls. Not only did this insure that everyone who wanted to vote could do so; it also provided moral support for the hundreds of Negroes who had never voted before, and for those who would have to depend on friends to tell them which boxes on the ballot to check because they could not read. In almost all districts, over ninety per cent of the registered Negro voters were at the polls an hour before they opened. There were many grim faces, and many laughing faces.

August 6 had been prepared for by almost two weeks of intensive organization. On that day of all days we anticipated violence, and volunteers were told to stay completely out of the way. If we had succeeded in convincing the Negroes to vote, taught them how to vote and how to protect their voting rights, if we had seen that they had made arrangements for getting to the polls, there was nothing much for us to do on that day. Most volunteers spent the day in the homes of Negroes who lived close to the polling places, prepared to take off for McFerren's store or the Memphis FBI office at a moment's notice. At McFerren's there was a pool of emergency aid: two law students, a number of students from Nashville who had come over to help for the day, and, of course, the field director.

Election day passed with few incidents. Two volunteers were shot at during the day, but neither was hit. In one district, the telephone wires were cut as we called our lawyer about violations, necessitating an auto trip to Memphis. In most polling places the white election officials were more polite than hostile, evidently not knowing what to expect from pollwatchers. With the eyes of the pollwatchers and the press on them, almost all districts put up some show of holding a fair, open election. And the Negroes did turn out, despite a few last-minute attempts to divert them. (A prosperous Negro bootlegger working for Pattat offered fifty cents extra per bushel for picking peas on election day, and he got a fair number of takers.)

From all the evidence, we felt justified in concluding that the whites had been led, or forced, to put on a show of at least token compliance with the election laws of Tennessee. In some cases their attempts to do so, because they were as inexperienced in running a fair election as the Negroes were in voting in one, were downright funny. Try as they might, they did not run a fair election that day; nor did they try as hard as they might have, as our later sampling of election day violations will attest. It was quite a day.

By noon all the Negroes except the schoolteachers had voted and gone home, excited and exultant, satisfied that they had done their part, gratified and amazed that there had been no violence against them at the polls, nor any suggestion of later reprisals. It was very hot that day, somewhat over a hundred degrees with the humidity close behind; and it was a very tense day for us all. We would not even begin to know the outcome until the polls closed. In the meantime, some of the volunteers had already begun to take down affidavits of the many violations of the day. The alternative was to chatter nervously, to stew in the juices of the climate and the occasion. Many took up both alternatives.

Chapter V

Aftermath

THE POLLS CLOSED at 4:00 in the afternoon and the counting began immediately thereafter. In several districts one or more Negroes were permitted behind the closed doors to watch the count, a gesture in the direction of fairness, but in this case a hopeless one; L. T. Redfearn and June Dowdy were defeated before the votes were counted. Returns began to come in by 5:00, and it was soon apparent that Redfearn had been defeated by a margin of nearly two to one.

We can never know exactly what happened, but many forces conspired to take the election out of the Negroes' hands. More than one ballot box had clearly been stuffed; in one case the reported vote for Pattat exceeded by a hundred votes the number of persons who had been counted voting. Illiteracy was the worst enemy of the Negroes who voted; many were confused by the printed ballot, which was different from the sample (based on the absentee ballot) we had distributed; many more were simply overcome by the problem of walking through a group of white "bossmen" and marking a ballot. In every polling place there were from twenty-five to fifty ballots which had simply been folded and placed in the box—blank. Many of the Negroes who had placed blank ballots in the box told us they did that rather than vote for Pattat. Illiteracy is a harsh tyrant.

Everybody was at McFerren's that night, the volun-

teers to report how the election had gone in their districts, and Negroes from all around the county who had worked for this election and felt the need to draw together. In retrospect, the volunteers could recall that as far back as March and the debate at Cornell, Haynie and others had stated that the chances of having a free election (much less a legal one) were slim indeed. But the weeks of mass meetings in warm, enthusiastic Negro churches, the strong, confident campaigns of Redfearn and Dowdy, and the rumors in circulation just before election day had lulled most of us into believing that if we could prevent major voting violations, Redfearn, and perhaps Dowdy too, would certainly be elected.

People wandered back and forth in front of the stores and traded anecdotes of the day. Charlie was on the phone all evening, calling Washington, Nashville, New York. Several reporters were still getting their facts straight. And over the whole warm nighttime scene, with its confusion of automobile sounds and jukebox music, there was a feeling of numbness. In the midst of all this aimlessness, Charlie seemed unbelievably calm. There was work still to be done; it was no time to indulge in anger.

There were affidavits still to be collected, affidavits of every kind, from pollwatchers, and from those who had stood outside the polling places counting, and from anyone who had voted. Whether or not we could take the election to court, these signed statements would be invaluable in appealing to the Justice Department and the press. All the pollwatchers who had been turned away when they presented their credentials had signed affidavits immediately; now began the enormous task of collecting a statement for every violation of election law we could find, from electioneering within fifty feet of the polling place to opening a Negro's ballot and reading it.

Friday morning (August 7) was spent in collecting affidavits and putting in order the notebooks which each team had kept during the summer. For each district there was to be one notebook, containing the names of all registered persons, the names of the road, section, and district leaders, maps of small sections showing where people lived, and other useful information pertaining to elections. Those who planned to leave that afternoon packed and began the difficult task of leave-taking.

Before anyone could leave, however, the project had agreed to meet for the last time as a group on Friday afternoon at Harris's picnic grounds. Mr. and Mrs. Harris had spread the word that they were giving one of their famous barbecues for the "freedom workers," and leaders from most districts were present. While our hosts were feasting on Mr. Harris's barbecued pork, the volunteers withdrew to a corner of the picnic grounds to discuss one vital question, how best to use the money left in the Fayette County Fund.

Each of the volunteers present at this last meeting had his own ideas about how some $4,500 might be used. Charlie's one stipulation was that $1,500 must be earmarked for the legal expenses of contesting the election. Two volunteers proposed that, since every member of the project had made a considerable personal sacrifice to spend the summer in Fayette County, any money left over should be divided among the volunteers themselves. This idea was immediately shouted down; most of the volunteers were convinced that, no matter how it was distributed, the money raised for Fayette County ought to be used there. The next conflict was over the problem of whether the money should be administered by the project to prevent the kind of infighting and jealousy that had occurred over the clothes and money which poured into the county in Tent City days, or whether it should be left in the hands of some organization of the Negroes themselves. If so, should it be divided equally among the election districts or handed over to the Civic and Welfare League or to its political arm, the Citizens' Committee? What about reserving some money to help pay the expenses of Fayette County children who might be able to go to school for a year in the North? Then there was also a need for money to finance a proposed "public library" in District 8, to bring educational films into the county, to finish the Community Center . . . and so on, *ad infinitum*.

Also, what about next summer? If some volunteers were to return next summer, or even expand the project to include literacy schools, shouldn't money be reserved for that? And it might even be possible to pay a small salary to keep one full-time civil-rights worker in the county throughout the year. As the discussion dragged on, it seemed at times that the proponents of the various schemes would never be reconciled. The final decision represented a compromise and was formulated by Charlie Haynie. Whatever money was left after the lawyer was paid and the expenses of contesting the election had been put aside, would be divided into three equal parts; one to be handed over the the Fayette County Citizens' Committee to use as it saw fit; one to be devoted specifically to the registration drive; and one to be administered at Cornell for the *ad hoc* needs of the project.*

The decision made, volunteers returned to their friends for the formal leave-taking. Speeches were made, as they always are in Fayette County, by anyone who might possibly have something to say. Each district reported on how its members had turned out for the election; the

* For example, some of this third was used to pay the expenses of three volunteers who returned to the county for several days before the presidential election in November.

three districts in which Redfearn had won were elated, but the others had encouraging news. Each ended on a note of hope which rang true: "Next time we know we can do better."

Finally Viola McFerren spoke, and this magnificent woman, who rarely allows herself to display emotion, had tears in her voice when she said, "I want to thank you all for helping us so. Before you all came down here, I was afraid for many things. It was hard for you to come so far from your homes, and hard for us to understand you. But I want you to know that we are your friends and you are welcome here any time you want to come back."

The speeches over, those who were leaving immediately said their good-bys, promising to write, to come back at Christmas, to come back next summer, to come back sometime. Those who remained would collect more affidavits and try to insure that the political machine we had helped create would not grind to a halt when the "white visitors" left.

The farewell picnic was on August 7. More than a few eyes were filled with tears that day, as we and our friends in the county realized that the closeness of the preceding several weeks was to be abruptly terminated —at least for a while. Since then, much has happened, some of it extending the achievements of the project, some of it revealing the need for continuing work by us in the county, and some of it pointing to the need for increased pressure on the state and national authorities to enforce the laws of the land. It will be convenient to discuss these matters in terms of three separate (but of course related) contexts: governmental response to election-law violations, the activities that have gone on in the county since election day, and the activities of the project members since their return from the county.

As mentioned earlier, part of election day was spent collecting affidavits of election-law violations, and that activity continued for a few days after the election, as a few volunteers stayed on for that purpose (and also, it may be said, because some were simply reluctant to leave). During election day Charlie had spoken on the phone to the Department of Justice in Tennessee and in Washington, to our lawyer in Memphis, who was seeking federal-court action during the day as violations piled up, and, in desperation, to Drew Pearson (with whom one of our volunteers had a connection), to see if Pearson's position might be able to bring action, all else having failed.

By noon, Pearson had begun to make phone calls himself. What ensued so outraged him that he devoted the entirety of his syndicated column on both August 11 and August 12 to our failure to get federal help. Following are some excerpts from his columns, which suggest the frustrations one can suffer simply by trying to have the government lock a barn door *before* the horse is stolen:

[After Haynie called me for the second time] I telephoned Burke Marshall, in charge of civil rights. He refused to take the call. I was told to talk to Edward Guthman, in charge of press relations. Mr. Guthman was out, busy publicizing Attorney General Kennedy, who in turn was telling Democratic candidates for Congress how to win the next election. I was then told to call Jack Rosenthal, his assistant. Mr. Rosenthal was out. I sent an assistant to Rosenthal's office. He was kept cooling his heels one hour. Meanwhile I called Gerald Jones in the Civil Rights Division. He was courteous, but referred me to John Murphy, Chief of Justice's General Litigation. He refused to take the call. Another call to Burke Marshall, head of civil rights, went unanswered. Finally I phoned the White House. . . . There, Lee White, in charge of minority problems, got busy immediately. He said he would get the FBI into the case.

Pearson went on to say that he continued to receive calls from Haynie, at 2:00 p.m. and again at 4:00 p.m., reporting more violations, and also that there was no sign of the FBI or any other governmental agents. Pearson continued:

At 5:00 p.m. Rosenthal phoned from the Justice Department to say that the FBI had gone promptly to Somerville. At 5:45 p.m. Haynie called to report that two FBI men had arrived from Memphis, and informed him that they were not there to provide any protection for election workers or to visit the polls [which, by then, had been closed for almost two hours] to check on election irregularities; but to interview only two people—John McFerren, leader of the local Negro movement, and [the] attorney for the group.

The latter had been in Memphis all day, trying to get the help of federal authorities. (The FBI and the federal courts are in the same building in Memphis.) The FBI agents from Memphis went to Somerville to speak to our attorney, who in turn had been trying to get them to speak to him all that day—in Memphis. They also wished to speak to McFerren—and nobody else—despite the fact that the latter was acting as a pollwatcher and would not be pulled from that duty, after all the years' work leading up to that election. So the FBI came out to the county, late, spoke to nobody, and left. That was as much as did that day. What has happened since?

When Haynie left the county, a few days after the election, he went immediately to Washington, to speak to those in the Civil Rights Division of the Department of Justice. Haynie was only one of several members of our group who subsequently made such visits. The visits had one thing in common—we were received politely, and the visits have been, at least to date, fruitless. There was one occasion that was shocking, if still handled politely. That was when Haynie and Tim Hall were told, six days after the election, by U. S. District Attorney Thomas Robinson, "Look, I can't get involved in every Susy Mae and Annie Belle's troubles." Fayette County is in Robinson's District, although he didn't think so. Nor did he know, until shown the law by Haynie, that federal law covered the violations we cited.

As a consequence of receiving little but polite evasions and vague promises from the Justice Department, Haynie set about organizing a protest. The form this took was twofold: letters to congressmen and the Justice Department, and a brochure briefly describing the county's problems and listing fifteen charges against the election officials of the county. The brochure was sent to newspapers, congressmen, and the Justice Department. It is worth listing some of these charges, not only to provide an efficient survey of the problems encountered in the attempt to have a fair election, but also to suggest the dimensions of the violations which have failed to move the Department of Justice.

1. All of the three hundred election officials were whites, even though Negroes make up about seventy per cent of the population and more than fifty per cent of the registered voters of the county. Some officials were at the time of the election under grand-jury investigation for assault-and-battery charges made by civil-rights workers.

2. Between five hundred and one thousand Negroes attempted to register for the August 6 election, and waited outside the office of the registrar on June 17, June 24, and July 1. They were not registered, because of illegal delays in the registrar's office.

3. An undetermined number of Negroes, perhaps over one hundred, were "registered" earlier in the summer, but found on election day that the registrar had listed their residences incorrectly on their permanent registra-

tion forms. They were not allowed to vote.

4. At almost every precinct in the county, some Negroes were ejected although they presented official papers designating them as pollwatchers for legally qualified "freedom candidates" in the county election. Some of the pollwatchers for Ross Bass, the successful candidate for the Democratic nomination for the United States Senate from Tennessee, were similarly ejected from the polling places. In one case a pollwatcher was arrested, apparently for protesting what appeared to him to be wholesale stuffing of the ballot boxes.

5. Bass pollwatchers who were admitted were prohibited from effectively watching the election.

6. At many precincts, Negroes were not allowed to witness the counting of the ballots, even though state law expressly provides that any voter may do so. White voters were allowed to watch the count.

7. At some precincts, whites were allowed in to vote ahead of long lines of Negroes, although many of the latter had waited for hours and despite the fact that the state law expressly forbids such actions.

8. At those polling places where a reliable count was made of the number of persons entering the polling place, including the election officials themselves, the total reported vote significantly exceeded the official count.

9. Officially designated polling places were altered, without prior notice or attempts to announce the change to Negroes standing in line at the originally designated spot. Also, officially designated times during which the election should have occurred were altered at some polling places.

10. Negroes attempting to write in the name of a local Negro for district constable were not allowed to do so, even though their procedure was correct and in accordance with their rights.

11. There were many instances of harrassment outside the polling places, of improper behavior by election officials, of automobiles transporting Negroes to the polls being intimidated and attacked by whites. Two of the volunteers were shot at by a white, whose identity was known.

The last official word concerning the plans of the Department of Justice regarding the foregoing (and other) violations was received in mid-November, 1964. It was in the form of a letter to Senator Javits (to whom we had written, seeking his assistance in obtaining the intervention of the Justice Department), which the Senator kindly passed on to the project chairman. The letter reads in part:

Neither this Department nor any Federal agency is authorized to supervise local elections. However, complaints that have been received about the conduct of the election are being investigated, and appropriate action will be taken promptly if it develops that a violation of Federal law has occurred.

The tone of the letter is polite; its contents are misleading. The election of August 6 was not just a local election; had it been, as the Department of Justice surely knows, candidates for the United States Senate would not have been running. The Department also knows that some of the violations were perpetrated against poll-watchers of a candidate for the senate office. Presumably, the Department also knows the contents of the Civil Rights Act of 1957, 1960 and 1964, the last signed into law five weeks before the election.

What are we to conclude about the apparent indifference to enforcement of the law by, of all agencies, the Department of Justice, Civil Rights Division? For those who work for civil rights in the South, who have friends who have been beaten and killed, who have informed previously discouraged Negroes that today, if not yesterday, they will be protected by the law, if only they will stand together—for such as these, it is difficult to control feelings of bitterness. It is difficult indeed; but those who work for civil rights must, and most do, control such feelings. We know, or we trust, that the Civil Rights Division is badly understaffed, and that if it has not moved at all in some areas, it is trying to move in some others. We know that its staff will be increased only by public demands to that end, and that its work will become effective to the degree that public support increases. Bitter or no, therefore, our task is left unchanged. It is nonetheless difficult to eradicate all suspicions that the federal government is doing somewhat less than it has the resources to do.

There were also feelings of bitterness in the county after the election, nor have they lessened with the passage of time. However, for residents of the county, as for us, the task was clear: keep working. A rundown of the activities in the county itself shows that the spirit of the summer still sings. Here are excerpts from letters received by some of us since August:

. . . Every Body doing verry well in health. We are doing fine out in the field of registering the peples and we are making some progress in school. We was at Mt. Zion on the railroad last night and we will be their Thirsday night. A lots of peples is comming to the school but it is a lots of things we need in school about politics to teach them. We dont have the proper books and can't get them. Some how if you got any idears how to get them let us no at once because we realy need something real bad so do what you can. . . .

. . . This leaves me fine in health, but a little tired, and so much work to do I can't rest. I just come from Somerville, this was the last day to register before the [November 3] election. We registered 73 today and on last Thursday 75 and 7 changed their address. Oh! yes we are working hard. We all were in Somerville today with a load of people, and I am almost sure everybody in Dist. 10 is hard at work. . . . I am so glad that you all in New York are thinking about us here in Fayette. You know when I get your letter today I was so glad today I just had to ans. it today I could not wait I had to write you, because I know we are not fighting this alone, and I just know we will overcome with friend like you and the others. Listen! We plan to go to some of the other Districts and try to build them up like Dist. 10. . . .

. . . We are doing find with our school I am thrilled so thrilled that I can't explain, and I am going to close for now I am pushed for time. . . .

. . . We go to Somerville every registration day, and stay all day from 8 in the morning until 4:30 in the evening. And believe me it is a good job, we have been there every week since Aug. 6. I keep a record of everybody that gets registered. Oh let me tell you about my school we have 35 people now attending our classes, many of them at first couldn't write their name and now they are able to write their name and to write a few other things. I let the kids and others teach them math and reading, and I teach them politics. By November they will know how to spell the name democrat and the name republican and they will know which ballot to choose. . . .

. . . Do you know that our registrar resigned now what do you think of that? We got in touch with the Justice Department also we went to WDIA [the Negro radio station in Memphis] and gave them a full report of what had happen and they made a newscast from it, as of now I don't know what will be the results of this little insodent. But I hope that it will not be long before the books are open again and we will start things of with a bang again. . . .

. . . [From a letter dated November 30] I have been to the register's office every Thursday, and last week. I went to

Somerville every day last week, but I didn't find out what days they registered. They are giving us the run around, but tomorrow we plan to go to attorney Mathews and ask him just one more time, and if this don't work we plan to let all the high authorities know that we can not get registered. I'll let you know What Happened. . . .

From these quotations alone, the following may be noted: registration is going on with determination on the part of the Negroes and jiggery-pokery by the whites; literacy schools have been started, and they teach both basic subjects and "politics." What may also be gleaned are the quite wonderful feelings that now tie us to the people of the county.

We were able to find a fine young woman, Deborah Rib (a friend of one of the volunteers), to go to the county in October for an indefinite period of time. Deborah is being paid a subsistence "salary" by the project, and she is providing valuable services of continuity and co-ordination for the project and the people in the county. Her presence made the return of three volunteers for the November 3 election more efficient and more fruitful; their return made it possible for us to know better what is now happening in various parts of the county.

There has been some falling off of energy devoted to politics, naturally. But the amount still so devoted is considerable, and it is being used in hopeful ways. In Fayette County, politics, literacy, and civil rights are merely different facets of the same thing, and the people in the county now act on that understanding. Perhaps one of the most encouraging developments is the now almost instinctive reaction of the Negroes to report any kind of irregularity to the Department of Justice—to fight back. (One thing we also know. If, sometime soon, seeking the help of federal government does not produce visible results, there will be a terrible demoralization for many fine people in the county.)

Some steps requiring our help have been taken since our departure. A library was begun in one of the districts, and we have been able to collect and ship about six hundred volumes for it. Two of the young people from the county are now attending school in New York State, at no cost to themselves. One (who lives with the family of one of the project members) is repeating her last year of high school, and hopes to go on to college either next year, or after one *more* year of high school (such being the value of a Fayette County education for a Negro). The other young person is taking courses in Binghamton, New York, and working while there, in the hope that he will be able to matriculate at college the following year. This year we are attempting to bring together families in the North and children from Fayette County, so that the latter (of high-school age) may live and study in the North for their last two or three years of high school. This is a delicate and complicated matter to arrange, but the prospects at both ends look promising. One girl, too, is taking an extra year and a half at a high school in Iowa, and has applied to Cornell for admission. If her school work goes well, she is likely to be accepted, with all financial requirements subsidized.

It was because of the developments just now suggested, and those discussed in earlier chapters, that the volunteers felt frustrated and dismayed, when they returned home, upon hearing the almost inevitable greeting: "Sorry the project failed." Those who greeted us in that manner did so with sympathy; many still cannot understand that all we lost was an election. In every other sense, in the deepest sense, the summer was a triumph. In the many meetings, articles, talks, and private discussions that have taken place at Cornell since the

summer, much time has been taken up trying to explain why we feel we didn't fail. We are still trying.

It is important to try to explain the virtues and problems of something like the project to friends who continue to be puzzled. It is also important to keep the project going, and many who are still at Cornell have contributed time and money to that end. When the three volunteers went down for about a week, around November 3, they pulled a trailer behind them, filled with books and clothing. The poverty of Fayette County has many sides to it, one of the most obvious being the dreadful state of the clothing worn there. In the summer, that is not too much of a problem—except that parents often refuse to let their children go to school, if they must go in rags. With winter coming on, we felt impelled to collect good used clothing, and were able to collect a good deal, with little effort. One trailerload was taken down late in the summer, another in early November, and there will be still a third at Christmas time, when a few of the volunteers return once more.

When the project was first developing, in the winter of 1964, the question was often raised, "Are you people just going to go down there, raise hell, and walk away?" Almost all of those who became volunteers would answer, as quickly as possible, "Of course not." But it is doubtful if many of us knew whether we meant what we said, or what we meant. Now we know. We are linked to our friends in the county. One of the three who went down for the November election expressed it best, if unintentionally. When the car stopped and he set foot in the county, he said, "I felt that I was home again."

Chapter VI

Next steps
and some reflections

So, WE LEARNED A LOT—about ourselves and our friends in Fayette County, about the struggle for civil rights both in the North and in the rural South. We learned that what is possible is not neatly circumscribed and fixed in its dimensions; the boundaries of the possible can be pushed outward by those who refuse to be captive to past and present. We learned, too, that good intentions and stout hearts do not guarantee against mistakes, some of them serious. We learned, therefore, something more about what is necessary, and what is desirable, in this kind of work.

A magnifying glass, when it catches the diffused rays of the sun and is focused properly, can set a haystack on fire, and that in turn may set whole fields ablaze; or the fire may fizzle, and burn out after igniting only a few straws. Right now, we know that the project set fire to a few haystacks—some at Cornell, and more in Fayette County. What the longer-run meaning of the project will be, cannot yet be known; it depends in part on how the breezes blow; in part it depends on how much heed is paid to experience, and how we build on it.

The project members learned a good deal about their individual strengths and weaknesses during the summer, and all discovered that they had both. Students who had often led a feckless existence before the summer found themselves responding with imagination, diligence, in-

telligence, and courage to the challenges of the county. Some who had been "cool" in their personal lives found unsuspected freshets of warmth moving in them, called forth by the great humanity and dire circumstances of our friends in the county. In short, there was a pronounced development toward maturity and greater identification with our fellow men, as we found ourselves lifted away from textbooks and placed down among the compelling realities of Fayette County.

This was so despite the diverse, in some cases perverse, motivations of those who signed up for the project. It is a commonplace that in the civil-rights struggle, as in other protest and reform movements, many who volunteer do so for the "wrong" reasons—whatever the "right" reasons may be. Some join up for excitement, some out of guilt; some for deep-seated political considerations, others out of simple curiosity; and still others in response to other "wrongheaded" impulses. Whatever the initial motivations of the members of our group, they were shoved aside very soon by a determination to right the wrongs of Fayette County. Those wrongs were so obvious, so substantial, so upsetting to see; the people of the county responded so quickly to the chance to move toward dignity and freedom, and placed such faith in us as their guides; we *had* to become the men they took us to be.

That we did not always succeed, that the frailities of some occasionally popped out, is to say no more than that one summer is not long enough to grow up, no matter what the conditions. We were of many ages, we made many mistakes, and of all kinds. In our enthusiasm to spur the determination of the Negroes to fight for their rights, a few of us portrayed the whites of Fayette County as little more than a pack of malevolent dogs. (When this happened, it is good to note, we were sometimes reminded by the Negroes that the whites were caught up in a social tragedy no less than they were themselves.)

There were other mistakes. Some of these were almost criminal in context; others merely echoed the persistence of childishness on the part of some, especially as regards the rules of the project. Despite the rules against weapons, at least two of the teams carried guns. One member of one of these was caught and arrested by the sheriff, and barely escaped a severe prison sentence. That in carrying weapons in the name of self-protection these volunteers were endangering not only themselves but the entire project was a lesson they had to learn—if they did —by hard experience.

On one occasion, the violation was massive, involving thirteen volunteers. It led to a disgraceful and dangerous incident. The summer was almost over, and everyone was tense, most were exhausted. A group of the volunteers went drinking in a neighboring rural county—neighboring both Fayette County and Mississippi. What ensued was a night of drinking and behavior that, whatever one might think of it in the North, was a disgrace to those participating, and a terrible danger not only to those participating, but also to the rest of us. Had the luck of those on the spree turned just a little sour, the night could have become one of violence and bloodshed, and the entire project might have been endangered in an attempt to rescue those breaking the rules. The rules had been explicit, they had been broken, and there seemed only one correct course for the leadership to follow. Most of the offenders were sent home the next day. In the process, the project was split wide open, and the precious energies of many of its members were wasted in bitter and useless debates over the incident and the decision. All this happened a few days before the election. Happily, the project had worked so well that the Negroes of the county could function quite effectively despite this episode.

That such things happened was in part the fault of those who committed the violations; in part it was a fault of the project's leadership. The leaders were responsible for not having convinced certain volunteers of the necessity for following the rules—or failing that, for not excluding them from the project. Earlier, it was said that we allowed the volunteers to weed themselves out of the project. We were too loose in carrying out this process. We still believe it to be the best means to choose a roster of volunteers, but we could have been more insistent about the rigorousness of the rules we adopted, and their importance. Had we done so, some of those who did violate the rules might have dropped out, or become convinced. As it happened, the offenders—some of them, it should be said, very effective as project workers—resorted to surreptitious, dangerous, and devious behavior. The entire project was simply lucky to be hurt as little as it was by such weaknesses.

The leadership of such a project is not easy. For one thing, guidance for the summer's work could not be gleaned from a manual; the basic tactics and strategy had to be developed on the spot. Secondly, the county is enormous, and under the most ideal conditions it would have been difficult to manage effective co-ordination. The conditions were far from ideal—only a few telephones, for instance, and those mostly tapped—and co-ordination was as evident in the breach as in the practice. There were only two full project-members' meetings during the summer. There should have been more. Had there been, at least one of the problems of the project might have been mitigated, namely, insistent mutterings that the leadership was acting in an arbitrary and secretive manner. The volunteers created many good things in the county; they also created many rumors, and these did much to make for unnecessary and harmful divisions. This problem was exacerbated by a third and unavoidable factor; by and large, such a project attracts not conformists, but individualists.

In this respect, the project's workings had the defects of its virtues. If it was too loose in some ways, at least it wasn't too tight. It was probably better to err in the direction of anarchy than of dictatorship, given the nature of the volunteers, and the problems of the county. Each of the fifteen districts of the county was in some important ways different from the others, if only in the differences found in the Negro leaders of the various districts. There had to be substantial diversity of technique and approach, and the district teams did very well in combining their own talents with the needs of their districts. Had they been forced to adhere closely to a set of rules worked out by one or two leaders, at the very least much time would have been wasted. The field director recognized this very soon and acted on it, perhaps too completely. There were some areas—involving information, plans, prospects, problems—where centralization and communication were much wanted. In a project of this sort care must be taken to see that someone is given the power and responsibility to perform such functions. All responsibilities must be clearly delineated; deadlines must be set, those responsible for meeting them made clear, and the deadlines must be met. To the degree possible, the structure of responsibility should be known to all, as should the area of individual discretion.

But that should not be construed to mean diffusion of authority. We found that when there was doubt as to the authority of the field director, confusion and chaos were the result. There must be one rule, on critical decisions.

That was our design; but the project members sometimes found it convenient to forget it. That cannot be allowed in a civil-rights project, least of all in the rural South. Such a project is like a small war, and individual egos must be subordinated to the cognizance of common danger. Where the line should be drawn between too much and too little centralization of authority doubtless has to be decided for each project; but it must be drawn, it must be made clear, and it must be accepted.

Some other things were learned, and these of a happier sort. The response of the Fayette County Negroes to our presence was most gratifying. Before the summer, many of us had feared that the Negroes would resent us, look upon us as patronizing outsiders come to use them as soap to wash away our guilt. We were wrong. Once our purpose was understood, we were embraced, protected, and loved. We were joined. As we grew, so too did the Negroes of the county; as we worked, they did. As we led, they became leaders. We were not water sucked into a dry sponge. We were water that nourished sprouting seeds. It will be pertinent here to give a few examples.

After one of our teams was chased and shot at, they were told by a sixty-year-old Negro, "Stop at my house anytime they're after you, day or night. We'll die together."

A Negro we called J. L., early in the summer told one of the budding Negro leaders that he was a fool to stick his neck out to work with us: "It won't do no good, and you'll just get killed. You can't change the world; you can't change much of anything at all." By election day, J. L. had been trained, voluntarily if with some caution, as a pollwatcher, the most dangerous thing a Fayette County Negro could be on election day. On that day, after the first pollwatcher had been ejected from the polling place—it was the same man J. L. had derided earlier—

J. L. went in and took his place. When he was ordered out by one of the fiercest racists of the county (a man known to have murdered several Negroes), J. L. stood his ground, saying, "I got my rights same as you." Finally, the white man got his gun and took J. L. away at the point of a gun. J. L. is now one of the strongest of the leaders in his district.

There were leaders in the county before our project was born, as may be deduced from its recent history. Now there are many more. One of these, a man of great energy and intelligence, had never lifted a finger for civil rights before June, 1964. At that time, in one of our small meetings, he volunteered to help. By the end of the summer, he gave the following talk to about two hundred of his people:

Some people are saying I'm going to get myself killed. Well, I don't think I'm going to get myself killed. But even if I did. At least I'll be killed while I'm fighting for my rights. We are all going to die. All of you will die in some way or another. Some of you will get sick and die, and some of you will get old and die, and a white man might come in his car and splash one of you on the highway. And you won't know why you die or what for. But I would at least know that I died while I was fighting for my rights. But I don't think they going to kill me, because they know it wouldn't do them any good. Because if they killed me, somebody else will come up and he will take my place, and then someone else to take his place, and so on and so on. But if something should happen to me, I want you to listen to me. There is something you can do about it now. You call the FBI. The *F B I*. They are in the phone book. You just call them. I tell you how to find the number. You just get the phone book and look and you will find it there. Look under *F B I*. You just call them and talk to them and they will listen to you, and they will come, too. You just tell them what happened to me, and they will come. But the white people know they will come, too, so they ain't gonna try to kill me.

All that from the man who knew that the whites had paid five hundred dollars to have him killed a few weeks before. We hear that the price has gone up to two thousand dollars now. He and another new leader in his district (the mother of twelve) are now going to night school in Memphis, to learn to read better.

Not only we and the Negroes of Fayette County learned and grew during the summer. Our young white lawyer from Nashville did, too. (He will be nameless here, for obvious reasons.) In what he says below there is revealed much that is important about the moderate white in the South, and some things to which attention should be paid by the moderate whites in the North. This is from a communication sent by the lawyer to us after the summer:

My first major surprise was the county itself. Coming from a city in Middle Tennessee, I was not prepared for the flat terrain, dry climate, cotton fields, sparsely-populated, racially-conscious area that existed in West Tennessee. . . . Being a native Tennesseean, this was probably more apparent to me than to the students from the other states, and where they could feel a large contempt for the uncivil bigotry as practiced in Somerville, I felt also a shame and inadequacy because this existed in my own state, and I had never even known about it, much less done anything about it. . . . The main thing that Fayette County needs is, I think, continued outside pressure. Even though the locals resent it, it is effective to continue their feeling that the Justice Department is telling them what to do.

What the lawyer has to say about the outside pressure reiterates one of the things we all asserted before; now we know it in our bones. The pressure must be kept on; and if it is, progress will be made. Progress requires pressure, in the South; and pressure means force. Here, as so often, it is essential to distinguish between force and violence. The federal government must force the

South to live up to the laws of the land. It must see to it that the laws are enforced, and it must announce that it intends to do so. Whether or not force leads to violence depends not upon the government, but upon those who would break the law. It is our conviction that violence in the South will be minimized by force, and increased without force. Negro and white civil-rights workers, from the South and the North, will not now stop their efforts; without governmental support, they will suffer violence.

The incidents of violence in our summer were without exception carried out by bullies; that is, they were carried out by those who always outnumbered the volunteers, and by those who acted assuming legal impunity. However, when the whites of the county—not least the sheriff and his deputies—saw that every incident was immediately reported to the sheriff and to the FBI, that whenever possible our people took down names, license numbers, and descriptions, that despite intimidation our volunteers continued to work in the same manner, then and only then they began to change their tactics.

After early July, violence in the county ceased. The three workers in Mississippi had been murdered, and the FBI had been called in. That made a dent on the whites in Fayette County. They knew that we would report all illegal actions, and that the individuals responsible were likely to be identified. The Negroes came to know this, too, and they too began to report incidents that customarily had gone unreported. This was why, toward the end of the campaign, Sheriff Pattat began to solicit Negro votes, to shake Negroes' hands, and to allow belief to grow that acts of violence could no longer be carried out with impunity. Whether the sheriff was worried for his own future as sheriff or possibly even as a prisoner (after numerous meetings with the FBI), or had received orders from the White Citizens' Council, or for some other reason, the county changed in that respect.

The election of August 6, 1964, was the closest thing to an honest election the county had ever enjoyed. Ballots were made out more or less properly, there were locked ballot boxes, pollwatchers were allowed in most places, and the Negroes stayed to supervise the counting at many polling places. There were no beatings, although the anger of the whites mounted during the day and led to some tense moments, and only a few Negroes were turned away at the polls. (However, one polling place closed, illegally, before a large group of Negroes could vote.) The whites did practice many frauds that day; but they were peaceful frauds. That marks progress for Fayette County. It is without doubt that the progress was an outcome of pressure and fear of further pressure from outside.

That was yesterday. Now we must plan for tomorrow. In addition to present activity in the county—the literacy schools, the new library, registration, various forms of continuing assistance to the Negro leaders—plans are now being worked out for the summer of 1965, with an eye also to the summer of 1966. Three of our volunteers plan to spend a year or more in the county, beginning early in 1965, to help develop and implement our plans.

There are two major jobs to be accomplished during the summer of 1965. One is for us to help in the drive for literacy, to give muscles and direction to the freedom schools already begun by the people in the county. Trained people are necessary, and the Fayette County Project is now recruiting a dozen or so such people to help out. A "trained" person in this context is someone who is studying or inclined to be a teacher. One of last summer's volunteers is presently developing the summer literacy project. He is a teacher at New York's Cortland State Teachers College (and also a Ph.D. candidate at Cornell). He, together with a literacy expert, will spend the summer in the county with ten or more volunteers.

The next steps toward political strength fairly cry out for our assistance. In the summer of 1965, L. T. Redfearn is likely to make another attempt to run for sheriff in the primary election. If he does so, he will both deserve and require assistance in bringing out the vote. Also, there is a good chance that district magistrates and constables can be elected fairly in the election of 1966, if the spadework is begun in 1965. Outside help is needed for such work. Thus, a dozen or so volunteers for literacy schools, another ten or so for political development—something like twenty volunteers will be recruited and financed for the summer of 1965. Some of the volunteers will be veterans of 1964; others will be new.

It is both imperative and feasible for the Negroes of Fayette County to move toward immediate desegregation of the public schools in the county, in keeping with the provisions of the Civil Rights Act of 1964. If they have not begun to do so by next summer, we shall help to plan the requisite steps. Ironically, were such an attempt to succeed—and there is little reason why it should not, now—the whites of Fayette County would be placed in the position of having to reconsider their position on federal aid to education. The principal opposition to such aid in the South has come because of the desegregation "problem." If desegregation is achieved *first*, there is every need and reason for federal financial aid to be sought afterward. The people of Fayette County cannot themselves finance an adequate school system *for all*, with or without segregation. Integration of the school system necessarily requires more good schools in the county; the ugly alternative, for the whites, is to have their children crippled in the grossly inadequate Negro schools.

And that raises the question of the long-run needs of Fayette County, Tennessee, and of much of the rest of the South. Except where industrialization is taking place, the South is too poor to support the number of people in it, white or Negro. In many senses, and in many of its parts, the South is still an underdeveloped area. Development programs are required to speed up industrialization where it is already taking place, and to extend improvement and industrialization to areas, such as Fayette County, where the need for economic stimulation from outside is desperate.

The TVA did this for much of Tennessee and surrounding states a generation ago. It changed the politics, the economics, and the social existence of much of Tennessee for the better; it barely touched Fayette County and then only through the wires that carry electricity, not through significant increases in employment opportunity. Jobs are badly needed. It need scarcely be added that the social and political changes of the civil-rights revolution in both the South and North will produce a hollow boom if they are unaccompanied by economic improvement. Nor should it be difficult to see that progress toward civil rights in the entire nation will be less abrasive to the degree that economic competition for jobs between white and black is reduced. The problem is already substantial, and growing apace.

Such steps, even were they to begin soon, would leave Fayette County afflicted with continuing long- and short-run problems. A glance at the eyes, the teeth, the bodies of both young and old in the county is all that is needed to reveal the need for a variety of programs—school lunch programs, and a daily allowance of milk for the children; a vitamin distribution program; health clinics for the Negroes; and, immediately, the introduction of plannedparenthood clinics. None of these programs would be new in the nation; all would be new in Fayette County. If there is a good reason why the governments of Tennessee and of the United States should not implement such programs immediately, it is not easy to see. The reason why they do not is, of course, easy to see, although it is not a good reason: Negroes have little or no political power. As their political strength grows, they may make some progress toward achieving benefits of the foregoing kinds; meanwhile, they and the other impoverished people of both South and North must rely on those who do have some political power to pressure governments along desirable lines. Such pressure would constitute a rewarding skirmish in the War Against Poverty, in addition to whatever else it might mean.

Whether or not the pressure to achieve civil rights and badly needed improvements succeeds will not be much determined by what the Fayette County Project has done or will do; it depends on the strength and dynamism of the entire civil-rights movement. Thus, our book ends where it began. Much more action is needed, now. Is it too much to expect that a few thousand more young and not-so-young people can enter the fight, immediately?

Is it so much to expect, say, fifty communities in this nation to develop new civil-rights projects in 1965? The civil-rights organizations listed in the Appendix have a list of needs so long that it could not sensibly be printed in this book; only its main outlines can be suggested. There are projects of all sorts, in all places, of all time durations: North and South, urban and rural, voting, teaching, slum improvement, fund-raising projects, for weekends, for weeks, for summers. There are so many kinds of needs that inability to find a project fitting one's own talents and possibilities cannot be used as an excuse for inaction.

Whether or not volunteers can be recruited and funds raised to finance the myriad projects, we are convinced, depends not on the inherent decency of the American people, nor alone on the merit of the projects. Let us assume the best—that there is a sufficient number of decent people—if only because to assume otherwise raises too many disturbing questions, suggests not only that we await a disastrous fate, but that we deserve it. Assuming the best, what then does it take to get those decent Americans to act, properly, enough, and in time? Not enough have acted, yet; that is painfully clear.

It has been the underlying rationale of this book that what "it takes" is a prodding process, that places in front of the decent person a collage that combines need, feasibility, and responsibility. Those who do not act when they see what they consider to be injustice, and when they know they are able to do something about it, are decent only in their vision of themselves; in no other way. It may be that something else is needed because of our way of life; namely, proprietary interest in those matters to which we lend ourselves. If so, that too can be arranged; that is what this book has been about.

It can be arranged by and for the young, the middle-aged, and the old. It can be arranged for all those who have up to now stood aside and worried, all those who wish now to step in and act—whether students or professors, businessmen or clerks, ministers, lawyers, or doctors. All are needed; all may serve. The ability and the inclination of students has been demonstrated; but should civil rights, should the permanent struggle for human decency, be confined to students? One of the four professors on the Fayette Project, a man of about forty, has explained his own participation. His words may help to free others to see their lives in a new light:

Several people said to me that since I have five children, I ought not to go—that was something for students, for young people. I really dislike this suggestion and all about it. I think it would be very sad if having a family (and I suppose, also, more to lose in the way of an established job, income, and so on) meant one thereby resigned, even *ought* to resign, from doing anything like this—would just leave it to the youngsters, those who had not yet "made it." It would mean that one would sanctify the idea of extended selfishness; morally endorse the notion that people ought to withdraw into their own families and the hell with things outside of them, if they might involve danger, or discomfort. That is just what I dislike so much, leaving dissent, dangerous dissent, to those who have little power and position. . . .

Who has the time? We all have some, to work in our own communities a bit every week, or in some other community for a few weeks, or a month. We all have different schedules, but are there any schedules that allow no wasted time? Can we afford to waste so much time, those of us who support the civil-rights movement, those of us who worry about tomorrow, those of us who can in speech and in feeling no longer tolerate the crimes of the past and present? Need we ask, in America, "Who has the money?" In America, for most of those who read these words, that question is much simpler than it seems. It should read, "Who, to achieve the dignity of himself and his brothers, can forego a bottle of Scotch, a new camera, a jaunt to Miami, even?"

All of us, of whatever age and station, have some extra time, some extra money. How many of us will cease depending on others—others, often, with less time, and less money—to do what we know cannot be done without us?

If not now, when?

If not you, who?

Appendix

Organizations and projects
seeking money and people

The listing that follows is meant to be suggestive, rather than comprehensive. It cuts across all kinds of civil-rights groups—religious, student, long-standing, new, action, study, fund-raising, and of course combinations of all of these and other types. The twenty-five groups listed actually stand for many times that number of functioning groups and potential projects, for some of them are centralized offices that provide information on a varied group of organizations throughout the nation. What have not been listed at all, with the exception of the Cornell group, are the numerous civil-rights organizations that exist at college campuses. Many of these organizations would provide a ready and excellent first step toward developing a project like the Fayette County Project. The next step might well be an inquiry to one of the organizations listed below.

By the time this is read, new groups may have come into existence and some of those listed may have expanded, contracted, or disappeared. The civil-rights movement is, of course, quite fluid, and consequently many of the groups that work within it have a mercurial existence. Some, unfortunately, are plagued by internal rifts—not least because their tasks are so much greater than their resources. The resources provided by newcomers will do much to strengthen existing organizations, as well as to broaden the base of the movement.

The first letter of inquiry, the first phone call, the first meeting seems to be the hardest step of all. It is also the most important step to take.

AMERICAN COUNCIL ON HUMAN RIGHTS
1130 Sixth Street, N.W., Washington, D. C.
A co-operative social-action program of five major sororities seeking to involve its members in the struggle to eliminate racial discrimination.

AMERICAN FRIENDS SERVICE COMMITTEE (AFSC)
1500 Race Street, Philadelphia, Pennsylvania
Offices scattered throughout the country. The AFSC has a wide spectrum of programs, operating in urban and rural areas. Other offices may be found in your local telephone book. Particularly well-developed community-relations programs, which focus on economic, educational and housing needs.

BAPTIST ACTION FOR RACIAL BROTHERHOOD, DIVISION OF CHRISTIAN SOCIAL CONCERN
American Baptist Convention
Valley Forge, Pennsylvania
A new group. Likely to have a summer project in 1965.

COMMITTEE FOR MINERS
1165 Broadway, New York, New York
Students worked with the Appalachian Committee for Full Employment last summer.

CONGRESS OF RACIAL EQUALITY (CORE)
38 Park Row, New York 38, New York
(Marvin Rich, Community Relations Director; Jim McCain, Director of Organization)
CORE has branches throughout the nation. Consult your local phone book. Its programs are quite diverse, ranging from demonstrations to sustained urban and rural projects. CORE projects have gone on and are planned to develop in areas as diverse as New York City, Chicago, Louisiana, and Mississippi.

CORNELL-TOMPKINS COUNTY COMMITTEE FOR
FREE AND FAIR ELECTIONS IN
FAYETTE COUNTY, TENNESSEE
P. O. Box 259, Ithaca, New York
(Douglas F. Dowd, Chairman)
The Fayette County Project continues. Funds and volunteers
for literacy and political projects in 1965 are still being
sought, both at Cornell and elsewhere.

COUNCIL OF FEDERATED ORGANIZATIONS
(COFO)
1017 Lynch Street, Jackson, Mississippi
Something like a funnel through which almost all civil-rights
activity in Mississippi pours. Participating organizations include the National Council of Churches, SNCC, CORE,
SCLC, NAACP, and others. COFO's summer project in 1964
is well-known. Those who wish to participate in it as individuals, or to form groups from their own area, should contact
the above address. Projects for next summer (1965) will
probably include attempting to work with poor whites, as a
program separate from the voter-registration and freedom-
school activities for Negroes. Information may be gained
about COFO from the participating organizations, especially
(for students) from SNCC offices throughout the nation. See
the citation for SNCC, below.

EAST HARLEM TENANTS COUNCIL
155 East 123 Street, New York 35, New York
(Ted Velez, Director)
The rent-strike organization. Volunteers and money both
badly needed, the latter for simple and obvious needs, the
former to help in various kinds of slum programs. Program
operates the year round; financial needs are most desperate in
the winter. A fund-raising program identifying your community with this program would be most helpful. Mr. Velez can
provide speakers and materials, within reasonable distances.
Wants to develop a summer program in 1965.

FELLOWSHIP OF RECONCILIATION
Box 271, Nyack, New York
Runs a variety of year-round as well as summer programs.

LEADERSHIP CONFERENCE ON CIVIL RIGHTS
704 Seventeenth Street, Washington, D. C.
Best place to call, for those in the Washington area.

NATIONAL ASSOCIATION FOR THE ADVANCEMENT OF COLORED PEOPLE (NAACP)
20 West 40 Street, New York 18, New York
Engages in court campaigns, educational programs, and selective buying campaigns, picketing, and direct-action programs. Field offices in San Francisco, Dallas, Atlanta, Philadelphia, Washington, Chicago, Baltimore, Boston, Detroit, Cleveland, Dayton, Pittsburgh.

NATIONAL CATHOLIC CONFERENCE FOR INTERRACIAL JUSTICE
21 West Superior Street, Chicago 10, Illinois
There are Catholic Interracial Councils spread all over the country. These councils operate in numerous ways to eliminate discrimination. The location of a CIC near you may be learned by writing to the above address, or by consulting your priest or phone book.

NATIONAL COUNCIL, EPISCOPAL CHURCH CENTER
815 Second Avenue, New York 17, New York
Education and action research in the area of interracial change.

NATIONAL STUDENT CHRISTIAN FEDERATION
475 Riverside Drive, New York, New York
This organization is for civil-rights purposes the same as the Ecumenical Volunteer Service of the National Council of Churches. It has information on church-sponsored civil-rights activities throughout the nation.

NATIONAL URBAN LEAGUE
14 East 48 Street, New York 17, New York

The League gathers and publishes facts about the conditions under which Negro citizens work and live. Program areas: job development and employment, education and youth incentives, housing, health and welfare, religious resources. Has local affiliates in about fifty cities over the nation. See your phone book.

NORTHERN STUDENT MOVEMENT (NSM)
119 Fifth Avenue, Room 302, New York, New York
(Paul Potter, President)

Purpose: to act as the main vehicle for action in the individual member campus groups, developing mostly tutorial programs, compiling background materials, and co-ordinating regional actions in the North.

PRESBYTERIAN SUMMER SERVICE AND
STUDY PROJECTS
United Presbyterian Church in the U.S.A.
825 Witherspoon Building, Philadelphia, Pennsylvania

This organization presides over a long list of summer service projects, including civil-rights projects (it was a participant in the Mississippi Project, 1964). Advisable to write to above address for the "Summer Service Packet, 1965," which is systematic and comprehensive.

SOUTHERN CHRISTIAN LEADERSHIP CONFERENCE
(SCLC)
334 Auburn Avenue, N.E., Atlanta 3, Georgia

Headed by the Rev. Martin Luther King. Nonviolent mass direct-action leadership training directed at the organization of communities at the grass-roots level; voter-registration workshops.

SOUTHERN CONFERENCE EDUCATIONAL
FUND, INC. (SCEF)
822 Perdido Street, New Orleans, Louisiana
(Rev. Fred L. Shuttleworth)

SCEF conducts educational workshops on a local and regional basis for the leadership of grass-roots civil-rights groups, and has several programs of its own, in existence or in prospect, including scholarship programs for deserving students, aid programs for victims of economic reprisals (which once helped those in Fayette County), a "job and freedom" program for Appalachia (which now seeks volunteers and funds), and so on. SCEF badly needs money for legal defense cases. SCEF's monthly publication *The Southern Patriot* is a most valuable source of information on the struggles and progress of the movement. Subscription rate is $2.00 annually, and well worth it.

SOUTHERN STUDENT ORGANIZING COMMITTEE
P. O. Box 6403, Nashville, Tennessee 37212

STUDENT NONVIOLENT COORDINATING
COMMITTEE (SNCC)
6 Raymond Street, N.W., Atlanta, Georgia
The most active of the student civil-rights groups. The listing for SNCC will be the longest here for that reason, and also because it has many programs, including "county-adoption programs" such as Cornell worked out for Fayette County, that lend themselves to the approach suggested in our book. County-adoption programs involve at least the following: the adoption of a county in, say, Mississippi, for exchange programs of students, food and clothing drives, exchange of ministers, and so on. Other programs involve the operation of freedom schools, construction and/or operation of community centers, voter-registration drives, and "federal programs" which center on legal analysis for use of field workers in areas such as Mississippi. There are also "support" programs of research carried on in the North, which provide useful information for those in the field or those more generally fighting for rights.
SNCC has a list of "Friends of SNCC Groups and Key Fund-Raising Contacts" for the entire nation, which it will provide on request. Write to the above address or the SNCC office at

1017 Lynch Street, Jackson, Mississippi. For Northern support work, write to SNCC Northern Co-ordinator, at the Atlanta address. There are offices elsewhere, but they usually refer all important inquiries to the Atlanta or Jackson offices.

STUDENTS FOR A DEMOCRATIC SOCIETY (SDS)
112 East 19 Street, New York 3, New York

Various programs, North and South, urban and rural. Many college chapters.

UNITED CHRISTIAN FELLOWSHIP—
DEPARTMENT OF CHRISTIAN ACTION AND COMMUNITY SERVICE
222 Downey Avenue, Indianapolis, Indiana

Summer service programs, for college-age youth, including, but not confined to, civil-rights programs.

UNITED STATES NATIONAL STUDENT ASSOCIATION (USNSA)
3457 Chestnut Street, Philadelphia, Pennsylvania

The Southern Human Relations Project of USNSA holds conferences and seminars in the South throughout the year, has conducted a voter-registration project in North Carolina.

YMCA AND YWCA
The YMCA and YWCA offices in your city can inform you of the existence and location of Social Action Committees of your denomination.

EU Authorised Representative:
Easy Access System Europe
Mustamäe tee 50, 10621 Tallinn, Estonia